Even When No One Is Looking

Fundamental Questions of Ethical Education

Even When No One Is Looking

Fundamental Questions of Ethical Education

Jan Hábl

FOREWORD BY
Thomas K. Johnson

CASCADE *Books* · Eugene, Oregon

EVEN WHEN NO ONE IS LOOKING
Fundamental Questions of Ethical Education

Cascade Books
An Imprint of Wipf and Stock Publishers
199 W. 8th Ave., Suite 3
Eugene, OR 97401

www.wipfandstock.com

PAPERBACK ISBN: 978-1-5326-3036-1
HARDCOVER ISBN: 978-1-5326-3038-5
EBOOK ISBN: 978-1-5326-3037-8

Cataloguing-in-Publication data:

Names: Hábl, Jan. | Johnson, Thomas K., foreword.
Title: Even when no one is looking : fundamental questions of ethical education / Jan
    Hábl ; foreword by Thomas K. Johnson.
Description: Eugene, OR : Cascade Books, 2018 | Includes bibliographical references
    and index.
Identifiers: ISBN 978-1-5326-3036-1 (paperback) | ISBN 978-1-5326-3038-5 (hard-
    cover) | ISBN 978-1-5326-3037-8 (ebook)
Subjects: LCSH: Ethics. | Moral education.
Classification: BL42 .H23 2018 (print) | BL42 .H23 (ebook)

Manufactured in the U.S.A.   SEPTEMBER 19, 2018

This book has been supported by the University of Hradec Králové, Czech Republic,
Comenius Institute of Prague and Giving Hands in Bonn.

Science editor: Dana Hanesová, PhD, doc.
Cover graphics: Adam Balcar

Contents

Contents

Foreword

You have in your hands a text by someone I take to be one of the very serious young moral philosophers of our time. The profundity of his analysis of the need for moral education reminds me of the style of analysis of one of the great moral philosophers of the final decades of the twentieth century, Alasdair MacIntyre. Hábl and MacIntyre share the persuasion that Western civilization has lost its way ethically on its journey through modernity and postmodernity, not in the limited sense that each of us is so much worse in our particular actions than our ancestors, but in the broader sense that as a group of cultures we have lost the ability to talk coherently about right and wrong. Both Hábl and MacIntyre are convinced that to address this deep-level moral issue we have to look to premodern sources of moral philosophy. But here Hábl and MacIntyre take different directions. MacIntyre thought that to escape the loss of a coherent perspective for morality we should turn to Aristotle (384–322 BC); Hábl recommends that we turn to Jan Amos Comenius (1592–1670). And, I have to say, I find Hábl's recommendation more compelling than the recommendation of MacIntyre because I find the moral philosophy of Comenius more compelling than the moral philosophy of Aristotle. That merits an explanation, keeping in mind that I am not attempting an independent interpretation of either Aristotle or Comenius, only a representation of how these premodern thinkers are interpreted by their recent protagonists.

MacIntyre concluded *After Virtue* (1981) with a haunting warning and exhortation:

> It is always dangerous to draw too precise parallels between one historical period and another; and among the most misleading of such parallels are those which have been drawn between our own age in Europe and North America and the epoch in which the Roman empire declined into the Dark Ages. Nonetheless

certain parallels there are. A crucial turning point in that earlier history occurred when men and women of good will turned aside from the task of shoring up the Roman imperium and ceased to identify the continuation of civility and moral community with the maintenance of that imperium. What they set themselves to achieve instead—often not recognizing fully what they were doing—was the construction of new forms of community within which the moral life could be sustained so that both morality and civility might survive the coming ages of barbarism and darkness. If my account of our moral condition is correct, we ought also to conclude that for some time now we too have reached that turning point. What matters at this stage is the construction of local forms of community within which civility and the intellectual and moral life can be sustained through the new dark ages which are already upon us. And if the tradition of the virtues was able to survive the horrors of the last dark ages, we are not entirely without grounds for hope. This time however the barbarians are not waiting beyond the frontiers; they have already been governing us for quite some time. And it is our lack of consciousness of this that constitutes part of our predicament. We are waiting not for a Godot, but for another—doubtless very different—St. Benedict.[1]

MacIntyre thought that men and women of good will must turn to construct new forms of community in which the moral and intellectual life can continue in light of the situation that the failure of the Enlightenment attempt to justify morality has left us in a new dark age. His description of that failure merits a summary; it is not too different from Hábl's description of the failures of modernity and postmodernity.

A quarter century after publishing *After Virtue,* during which MacIntyre patiently listened to his critics, he released a short summary of his main contentions in the preface to the third edition (2007). After noting that he had not seen any arguments that required changing his central contentions he wrote,

Central to these was and is the claim that it is only possible to understand the dominant moral culture of advanced modernity adequately from a standpoint external to that culture. That culture has continued to be one of unresolved and apparently unresolvable moral and other disagreements in which the evaluative and normative utterances of the contending parties present a problem of interpretation. For on the one hand they seem to presuppose a

---

1. MacIntyre, *After Virtue,* 263.

reference to some shared impersonal standard in virtue of which at most one of those contending parties can be in the right, and yet on the other the poverty of the arguments adduced in support of their assertions and the characteristically shrill, assertive, and expressive mode in which they are uttered suggest strongly that there is no such standard. My explanation was and is that the precepts that are thus uttered were once at home in, and intelligible in terms of, a context of practical beliefs and of supporting habits of thought, feeling, and action, a context that has since been lost, a context in which moral judgments were understood as governed by impersonal standards justified by a shared conception of the human good. Deprived of that context and of that justification, as a result of disruptive and transformative social and moral changes in the late middle ages and the early modern world, moral rules and precepts had to be understood in a new way and assigned some new status, authority, and justification. It became the task of the moral philosophers of the European Enlightenment from the eighteenth century onwards to provide just such an understanding. But what those philosophers in fact provided were several rival and incompatible accounts, utilitarians competing with Kantians and both with contractarians, so that moral judgments, as they had now come to be understood, became essentially contestable, expressive of the attitudes and feelings of those who uttered them, yet still uttered as if there was some impersonal standard by which moral disagreements might be rationally resolved. And from the outset such disagreements concerned not only the justification, but also the content of morality.[2]

Clearly, MacIntyre understood the Enlightenment as a philosophical catastrophe which led to entirely incompatible theories of ethics, such as Kantian, utilitarian, or contractarian, which led to entirely different and incompatible claims about the content of morality. The natural result has been emotivism, the deconstructive claim that any assertion about what is right or wrong is nothing more than an expression of emotions from the person making the claim, not much more than "I like it" or "I dislike it," whether one is discussing justice or genocide. In his critique of modern moral philosophy he concluded,

When Nietzsche sought to indict the making of would-be objective moral judgments as the mask worn by the will-to-power of those too weak and slavish to assert themselves with archaic and

2. Ibid., ix–x.

aristocratic grandeur, and when Sartre tried to exhibit the bourgeois rationalist morality of the Third Republic as an exercise in bad faith by those who cannot tolerate the recognition of their own choices as the sole source of moral judgment, both conceded the substance of that for which emotivism contended.[3]

MacIntyre contends that what was lost, and that to which Western society must return, was the conception of virtue and human nature found in Aristotle's *Nicomachean Ethics*.

> Within that teleological scheme there is a fundamental contrast between man-as-he-happens-to-be and man-as-he-could-be-if-he-realized-his-essential-nature. Ethics is the science which is to enable men to understand how they make the transition from the former state to the latter. Ethics therefore in this view presupposes some account of potentiality and act, some account of the essence of man as a rational animal and above all some account of the human telos. The precepts which enjoin the various virtues and prohibit the vices which are their counterparts instruct us how to move from potentiality to act, how to realize our true nature and to reach our true end.[4]

It is within this conception of humanness, he contends, that Christian, Jewish, and Muslim theologians wrote about right and wrong. And such theological conceptions only added to but did not fundamentally change the underlying conceptions of human nature and virtue.

> The precepts of ethics now have to be understood not only as teleological injunctions, but also as expressions of a divinely ordained law. The table of virtues and vices has to be amended and added to and a concept of sin added to the Aristotelian concept of error. The law of God requires a new kind of respect and awe. The true end of man can no longer be completely achieved in this world, but only in another. Yet the threefold structure of untutored human-nature-as-it-happens-to-be, human-nature-as-it-could-be-if-it-realized-its-*telos,* and the precepts of rational ethics as the means for the transition from one to the other remains central to the theistic understanding of evaluative thought and judgment.[5]

3. Ibid., 22.
4. Ibid., 52.
5. Ibid., 53.

With the rejection of Aristotelian teleology during and following the Enlightenment, the West was doomed to see all moral claims as little more than the expression of someone's will to power. The title of MacIntyre's chapter 9, "Nietzsche or Aristotle," nicely summarizes both his critique of the history of Western ethics and his proposal for the future. A return to virtue ethics, something like that proposed by Aristotle, is the only alternative to moral nihilism.

It is at this point that I wish to depart from MacIntyre's account and suggest that Hábl, or better Comenius as interpreted by Hábl, offers a more compelling account than Aristotle as applied by MacIntyre. Both visions include reviving some version of a religious/classical synthesis, a joining of key moral motifs from classical philosophy with themes from the theistic faiths, as a way out of the moral catastrophe of late modernity. This makes the two philosophical-moral projects profoundly similar; but there are also profound differences between the two proposed solutions.

One of those differences is the relation between a historical religion and the methods of moral analysis derived from classical Western philosophy; MacIntyre claims that the different theistic faiths developed their perspectives on ethics within a shared Aristotelian understanding of humanness, whereas Comenius as interpreted by Hábl applies methods of analysis derived from classical philosophy within a narrative derived from the Bible. This seems to be indicative of different approaches to the relationship between religion and philosophy, a difference that might be described as philosophy within the framework of faith (Comenius) versus faith within the framework of philosophy (MacIntyre). For MacIntyre, the Aristotelian teleology of the human seems to provide an authoritative understanding of humanness within which particular religious motifs are appropriated. One could be forgiven for wondering if MacIntyre's philosophy has become the queen of the sciences which rules over his theology, though phrasing the question in this manner may be overly hostile towards his intent. In contrast to this interpretation of MacIntyre, when we read Comenius, very clearly his biblically derived understanding of humanness and of the universe provided the authoritative framework within which he appropriated selected themes from different varieties of classical philosophy. I am tempted to say that MacIntyre proposed a renewed classical/religious synthesis as the solution to the moral crisis of late modernity, whereas Hábl is proposing a renewed biblical/classical synthesis as a solution to the moral crisis of late modernity, in both of which formulations the first term has the upper hand as the conceptual authority.

A second way in which Comenius as interpreted by Hábl is very different from *After Virtue* is what key themes and sources from classical philosophy are appropriated. As you will discover in this book, Comenius made extensive use in his ethics and pedagogy of much of what Aristotle taught about the unfolding of human potential toward its natural telos by means of the acquisition of virtue. Indeed, I suppose that Comenius would simply say "of course" to most of what MacIntyre writes when MacIntyre moves into a prescriptive mode of discourse, that of pursuing the moral and intellectual virtues in intentional communities. But there are also other themes from classical antiquity to be seen in Comenius as applied by Hábl which seem to be lacking in Aristotle as appropriated by MacIntyre, themes coming from both Plato and from the Stoics.

Hábl quotes C. S. Lewis, "A man does not call a line crooked unless he has some idea of a straight line." This is a means of reasoning which Plato used in his teaching, and it is, I believe, crucial to recovering from some of the worst symptoms of late modernity. Even if we cannot point to a single physical example of a perfectly straight line or a perfect circle, we have such ideals in our minds, and such ideals are important for teaching mathematics. More important for ethics and ethics education, even if we cannot point to perfect human examples of justice, loyalty, or kindness, we find such ideals in our minds. Hábl has done us the favor of appropriating this theme for our time, a theme which was not emphasized by MacIntyre.

At another point in his discussion Hábl claims, "The point is that the voice we hear within ourselves is real—it's our awareness of the moral law. It is part of being human: it's with me, in me, it's my conscience. If we didn't have one we would have no need of defending ourselves when we act against it." This a very Stoic way of reasoning, similar to what I would expect to find in some of the Roman Stoics such as Cicero and Seneca. It is part of what was rejected or ignored by the Enlightenment, part of what we need to recover in our day, another theme that was not emphasized by MacIntyre.

This way in which Comenius as applied by Hábl easily incorporates selected themes from multiple sources in classical Greek and Roman ethics and pedagogy into a broadly biblical narrative of the human condition has solid precedents. It is a pattern of ideas to be found in many of the great thinkers of the West, at least from Augustine through Aquinas, with other examples in the Christian tradition reaching back to Justin Martyr and in the Jewish tradition back to Philo, with successors to be found among some of the Protestant Reformers. And what is unique in all of this is that Comenius was continuing and developing this great tradition during the onset of modernity with a view to addressing the deep moral and educational vacuum made evident by the Thirty Years War (1618–1648). We must never forget that Comenius discussed his fundamental moral and educational philosophy with Descartes (1596–1650), the proto-typical representative of modernity and the Enlightenment. Comenius immediately perceived that Descartes was moving in a truly different direction philosophically. And, I am convinced, the direction set by Descartes led, in due time, to the complete loss of direction in ethics and pedagogy which MacIntyre has described so eloquently.

So read Hábl very carefully. He is a very serious moral philosopher with a very serious proposal for steps out of the moral confusion of late modernity, many of which should lead to steps in planning curricula for moral and civics education. Hábl is one of the voices to whom we have to attend if we wish to be something other than barbarians.

Thomas K. Johnson, PhD
Religious Freedom Ambassador to the Vatican from the
World Evangelical Alliance Global Scholars Professor
Research Vice President, Martin Bucer Seminary and Research Institutes

Introduction

Where Humanity Is Heading,
and What That Has to Do with Ethical Education

IN 2004, BASED ON taped telephone conversations, a Czech soccer referee was convicted and fined for accepting bribes to blow his whistle in favor of the team who paid him. The police had a suspicion for some time, and they secretly followed and monitored him and other people potentially involved. In the telephone conversations we can hear the desperate club director promising various sums of money if the referee would do it, because it was supposedly their only chance to stay in the league, and so on. We also hear the ref willingly giving responses like "Sure, you'll see on Sunday." When the police had enough evidence, the jig was up. What is instructive about this story, and relevant to the theme of this book, is the reaction of the referee. He immediately claimed that the behavior of the police wasn't "fair" (a beautiful sports term) because he didn't know his phone was being tapped. After a while, when he'd had time to think it out, he went back to the Strasbourg International Court with a counter-suit against the Czech Republic for allowing the police to act illegally. In addition to an acquittal he demanded financial compensation.[1]

A story like this is not unique, nor is it by far the worst one morally. From the many cases with which we're inundated every day I chose this one to serve as a starting point for questions of ethics. What is the essence of the concept of "fair," a word meaning "decent, honest, right"? What does the

1. Basic information about the case is available online (1. 10. 2015) at http://fotbal. idnes.cz/strasbursky-soud-prozkouma-korupcni-aferu-v-ceskem-fotbale-plo-/fotbal. asp?c=A090330_095250_fotbal_rou.

concept of "legal" mean? What is the difference between lawful and right behavior? What is justice? Where does moral or ethical awareness come from? What constitutes the concepts of good and evil?

This book is not going to include an inventory of ethical theories. They have been thoroughly treated by others.[2] Nor is it a detailed methodological-didactic manual for individual teaching units, theme-based, or age-based curricula, although a certain pedagogical framework will be outlined.[3] As the title indicates, it is primarily a search for the foundations or fundamentals upon which an ethical or moral education stands, and without which such an education would not be possible.[4] My intention is to formulate and rethink the basic questions that necessarily precede any kind of moral-educational action. What allows us to talk about good and evil? Is it possible to teach (or learn) virtue? What is the effect of our good—and bad—behavior? What does it have to do with human nature? Are we basically good? Or evil? What constitutes and legitimizes a teacher's moral supervision or training of another person? And how do we ensure that we get the desired result? What exactly is the goal of moral education? What does a morally educated, that is, a "good" person, look like? Or, in the words of Jan Amos Comenius—how can we teach a person to know the good, desire the good, and do what is good, and do it "even when no one is looking"?[5]

The answers to these questions form the outline for this book. Before I get started, however, it's necessary to make one methodological note. Ethical education is essentially a philosophical problem, and questions of morality or ethics are notoriously controversial. Not so much in content as in status;

2. See e.g., Příkaský, *Učebnice*; Anzenbacher, *Úvod*; Brázda, *Úvod*, Nullens and Michener, *Matrix,* among others.

3. For a thorough, methodological processing of ethical education see, e.g., Lencz and Křížová, *Etická výchova*; Nováková, et al., *Učíme.*

4. The concepts "ethical" and "moral" differ etymologically, but in normal usage they are synonyms. In this text, however, I will use them only as attributes of specific pedagogical activities oriented towards development, the so-called affective components of personality. While in the Czech Republic it is usual to speak of an "ethical" education, Anglo-Saxon literature speaks of a "moral" education. We will see that Comenius discussed "ethical" education in the same sense in which we today speak of a "moral" education. Therefore, I will not distinguish the terms in this work.

5. Comenius often repeated the triad: know, act, want (or love, or vote); see for example his *Pampaedia* I:9, IV:16. For the statement "even when no one is looking" see *Svět mravní*, the chapter on *Etika*, the section *O ctižádosti* (Comenius left this book unfinished, the notes and numbering of paragraphs are fragmented and confusing, therefore I have written out the reference.) See also *Obecná porada*, 570).

that is, in the justification of its moral basis or system—in short, we usually know how to behave, but we don't know why. From time immemorial we have argued about it—whenever we have taken the pain to think about it at all. I do not intend in this book to hide my philosophical standpoint under the guise of "academic" neutrality or the distance of a researcher. Nor am I going to feign some sort of godlike perspective offering a knowledge which claims it knows everything. Every person is an interpreter of reality, including moral reality, and every interpretation necessarily flows out of a certain philosophical pre-understanding, whether the interpreter is aware of it or not. Thus, every pre-understanding has its possibilities and limits, and therefore it's good to reflect on them and enter into dialogue with other pre-understandings. This usually results in mutual enrichment, inspiration and enlightenment. But of course, we must also acknowledge the unpopular philosophical fact that both good and bad pre-understandings do exist. For the bad ones we use labels such as prejudice, bias, partiality, etc.[6] Naturally we want to avoid such approaches.

I believe this text will be more understandable if I lay my methodological cards on the table from the outset. The questions I raise in this text aren't asked haphazardly, but they come from a position of traditional ethical realism.[7] In other words, I'm convinced that the moral categories have a real point of reference, i.e., they refer to reality, they are not merely constructs, whether they be epistemic, linguistic, social, psychological, or other. This central theme of the book I will expound later. However unnecessary this definition might seem, I believe it is important to articulate the foundations because so many of the ideological movements of our time are characterized by their ability to cast doubt on, in a sophisticated way, even the unquestionable, i.e., often even themselves, as we will see.

Why an ethical education?

"Why" questions don't have much place in the educational sciences. It seems to be a side effect of modern thinking, which has redirected the focus of human questions instead to the methodological "how." In the context of the Enlightenment paradigm of human autonomy it's an understandable

6. Prejudices acquired by every young generation in the so-called process of cultural transmission can be racial, ethnic, national, or religious. Zilcher and Říčan, "Multicultural," 194.

7. Cf. Sokol, *Etika*.

phenomenon, as the time was preoccupied with itself—how to be more advanced, more enlightened, more civilized, more progressive, etc. The development of new techniques and technologies facilitated better communication, travel, manufacturing, medicine, as well as "better" ways to kill, but there was never time to ask "why." Nor was there any reason to ask whether all the new scientific achievements were necessary, whether people wanted them, or whether they were worth the price. Why ask questions about meaning or goals when we have had such undeniable "progress," which has gradually become an end unto itself, justifying all means?

Modern pedagogy has been part of the story. It has spent the last hundred years desperately trying to keep up with the times, and failing, while at the same time ignoring questions of whether it's even a good thing to do it, and if so, with which time it's best to keep up. Reform follows reform, theoreticians and practitioners of education are working hard at coming up with ever more effective strategic methods, the empirical sciences supply pedagogy with technical refinements of every kind, research is overflowing with "how to" applications (many of which are pretty good), but the desired result of a versatilely developed, sophisticated humanity never appears. Yet the "why" questions are still not popular or common. Teachers cannot allow such a luxury, as they must invest all their time and energy in maintaining their teaching credentials—keeping up their communicative, methodological, organizational, diagnostic, and other skills. And with the advent of postmodernism the situation hasn't improved much; to the contrary, it has regressed. Teachers must constantly renew their entire pedagogical arsenals to undergo tests of hermeneutical doubt and at the same time adapt them to the nearly impossible requirements of public demands. And above all they have to pay attention to the marketability of their products, because the god Profit asks his due.

I am convinced that the crisis of the modern paradigm, which today's world is so intensively experiencing, can serve for the good. We thought that we knew "how to," but it has been shown that we didn't. We hoped that moral refinement would flourish along with intellectual knowledge and science, but it hasn't. We believed that the more one knows, the more humane they will become, but it turns out it is more complicated than that. The breaking-up of illusions is never pleasant, but if it brings as a by-product a certain amount of intellectual humility and a willingness to once again pose the basic questions of what exactly we are doing and why, then it has value. The pedagogical "why" always precedes and determines the resulting "how."

It would therefore be a mistake to skip or ignore those questions. Humanity intuitively resists meaninglessness, and naturally desires to know the reason why it does what it does. Moral educators are no exception. Therefore, it is the goal of this book to deal with those fundamental questions, as well as the foundational tenets of ethical-formative endeavors.

Chapter 1

Neither Angels Nor Demons
Who Are We, That We Need Educating to Be Good?

HUMANS ARE RATHER STRANGE beings. As opposed to every other thing in our world, a human nature or essence isn't given ahead of time as, for example, an earthworm is given its earthwormness or a circle its circularity. A circle can't do anything about its roundness, it can't become less round, nor can it develop into something more round. But a human being can. A person can become human or inhuman.

We are indeed special beings. We are capable of overwhelmingly beautiful and noble things, we're able to create, write poetry, or to sing in a way that gives life to another. We can not only desire, think, explore, and invent, but the power and depth of our thoughts and discoveries are overwhelming. Furthermore, we can laugh, rejoice, love, reach out to another, be courageous, be selfless, even self-sacrificing. We can forgive, be reconciled with another, help others, return a lost wallet with everything still in it . . . fascinating! Our philosopher forefathers said that it's because man is a spiritual being. The three basic spiritual qualities that separate him from the animals or mere matter are reason, will, and emotions. That is, the ability to appreciate and be touched by truth, goodness, and beauty.

People are odd beings, in which extraordinary nobility contrasts sharply with extraordinary depravity. They can be evil, and not only sort-of-by-the-way when they miss a goal, or fail at something, etc.—but truly and completely intentionally they are shown to have evil designs, to want evil, to be evil-minded. People are capable of meanness, lust, spite, cowardice, infidelity, ruthlessness; they are proud, rude, selfish, they know how to

1

very cleverly lie, steal, cheat, wound, rape, invent machines of torture—despite knowing how much it wounds and hurts—and even take the life of their neighbor. Most astonishing of all is that they often enjoy their own depravity. As G. K. Chesterton said, "man [sic] is the only being that can experience a very special and exquisite pleasure in skinning a cat alive."[1]

A human is an unusual being. "Corruptio optimi pessima"[2] goes the wise old saying, because there really isn't a worse thing than the combination of genius with evil. The greater the potential, the greater the benefit if it's actualized positively—and the greater the horror if otherwise. The potential of man is immeasurable. Is it possible to morally corrupt ants or earthworms? If it were possible there would clearly be a problem. But no one can equal a human being in intellect, creativity, imagination, resourcefulness, will, and the many other capacities that make them at once the greatest and the most abysmal creatures under the sun. The practical consequences of the ambivalence of human nature are tragic, and yet we often make jokes about our various human failings. We laugh at our own humanness; we think it's ridiculous. But earthworms don't laugh at their earthworm-ness. They don't find anything funny, or tragic, in it. Only people can—and sometimes have to—laugh at themselves. Or cry, or (often) do both at the same time.

We humans are remarkable beings. Neither angels nor demons. Angels are perfectly good, demons are perfectly evil; but among humans you don't find such extremes. In human reality we are more likely to encounter a loving and hard-working father of a family, whose character includes wide-ranging potential as well as various debasing tendencies like, for example, selfishness, or a desire for power—it doesn't have to be a lot of power, just a little is enough, maybe only within the family, or at the office or elsewhere. Or we might live next to a nice, decent neighbor, the greatest expert in automobile electronics in the whole area, kind, happy, wouldn't hurt a fly, yet allowing his own humanity to be crushed by his uncontrollable desire for alcohol; or by the greed which prevents him from reconciling the broken relationship with his brother over their inheritance; or by his relationship to the television which completely takes over all his free time and which, over the years, dulls his mind; or his relationship to social media, or to work, or to something else. And thus, from the old anthropological concept of *animal rationale* there remains only *animal*.

1. Free paraphrase from Chesterton, *Ortodoxie*, 12.
2. "The corruption of the best is the worst of all."

A person is a peculiar being. The inconsistency of human nature is so mystifying and unsettling that we often resort to various shortcuts or evasive maneuvers. For example, it would be a lot more bearable if human good and evil could somehow be neatly localized—be it in space or in time: good here/evil there, us/them, east/west, modern/ancient, the enlightened /the unenlightened, believer/pagan, angels on the left/demons on the right. Then it would be clear, nicely predictable, black and white.[3] But with people it's more complex. In them, good and evil dwell together. A human being is a "living oxymoron," as Peter Kreeft nicely puts it, "noble depravity, depraved nobility."[4] "We are an enigma to ourselves," adds Thomas Morris, who says we are the greatest mystery within us. How can one and the same creature produce such indescribable beauty and at the same time such incredible deformation? How is it that one and the same being can carry the potential for such wonderful good and such appalling horror? How can unprecedented kindness be wed to unheard-of cruelty in the same being?[5] Blaise Pascal writes similarly in his immortal anthropological meditations: "What a chimera then is man! What a novelty! What a monster, what a chaos, what a contradition, what a prodigy! Judge of all things, imbecile worm of the earth; depository of truth, a sink of uncertainty and error; the pride and refuse of the universe!"[6]

It is worth noting that we love our ambivalence. When some author manages to create a "good" character—whether in a book or a film—the hero is in some way good or brave or courageous, but also has some flaws. And we love those heroes because we can recognize and identify with them. And even when the author's strategy is the opposite—the hero is a villain (*Despicable Me*) but in key moments shows compassion or tenderness, we also love them, or at least sympathize with them. This is true even when the "hero" is a serial killer or psychopath like Dexter. However, if the hero is perfect—positively or negatively—the critics (and not just the professional ones) say it is "flat," "simplistic" or "not believable." To put it another way,

---

3. Still another popular strategy for comparing the ambivalence of human nature is the method of dividing people into categories of tangible and intangible, that is, body and spirit (or intellect), with everything positive usually ascribed to the spirit and everything negative to the body. Subsequently a blind eye is turned to one or another aspect of human nature, or it is downplayed or ignored, etc.

4. Kreeft, *Choices*, 55.

5. Thomas V. Morris, *Making Sense of It All: Pascal and the Meaning of Life* (Grand Rapids: Eerdmans, 1992) 129.

6. Pascal, *Pensées*, frag. 434.

we remember the names of Shakespeare's humanly flawed characters like Hamlet or Othello, but we can't remember the names of characters such as, for example, Dolph Lundgren, because none of those perfectly good or bad heroes are worth remembering. (In case you don't know who Dolph is don't worry, just forget this illustration.)

Who exactly is a human being? Who should one be? Why? And how? How should a person become who he or she should be? The ambivalence of human nature literally calls for an explanation. However diverse the answers may be, one thing is certain if only by intuition—if a person is to become fully human, it will never happen without effort. Humanity is not a fait accompli, it is not a given. Rather it can be understood as a task, a calling, or a mission which indeed calls a person, encouraging them to realize their potential, i.e., to fill their humanity with something valuable, noble, and dignified, and thereby prevent the atrophy which every dimension of humanity necessarily suffers if neglected.

It is this typical incompletion of human (moral) nature which gives meaning to moral education. If we were complete—perfectly good as the angels, or perfectly evil like demons—neither moral nor any other kind of education would be necessary. But for us human beings whose humanity oscillates our whole lives between conflicting poles and tendencies, moral education is irreplaceable. In addition to other factors it can become one of the major, if not the key activity to help people to discover and realize the potential of their nature, that is, it can help them become who they should be.

But who ought I be? What an extraordinary requirement: *ought, oughtness*. Requires who? Says who?

Chapter 2

How I Am and How I Am to Be

Is Human Being Good, or Evil?

THERE IS A DIFFERENCE between what is and what is to be. Anthropologically, there is a way I am, and a way I am to be. How is this possible? It is because human nature (essence) is complicated and complex on at least two levels—ontological and moral. In our being, ontologically, we are undoubtedly good, as well as dignified, valuable, noble, meaningful. We each are somebody. However, in our moral capacity we are ambivalent—capable of both good and evil. And not only capable, we all do good and evil deeds.

The ontological dignity of the human person has traditionally been justified metaphysically—from Moses through Plato, Aristotle, and Aquinas to Comenius. In one way or another people are perceived as beings who don't belong to themselves, but are related to something beyond themselves. And this "belonging" does not represent some kind of incidental or optional psychological need (as in wanting to have, or to belong to, someone), but it is an ontological status without which humanity lacks something essential.[1] It is the *nexus hypostaticus*, said Comenius, for example; that is, a person's essential relationship to the sacred. A person is someone because he or she is created as *imago Dei*, that is, in the image of God.[2] All of our personal capacity—the ability to know (ourself), to feel, to distinguish between good and evil, the beautiful and the ugly, the ability to love and laugh, etc.—was given to us in order to both enjoy it and to reflect it, and thus to honor the Creator as the *summum bonum* (the highest or greatest conceivable good).

1. Cf. Nullens and Michener, *Matrix*, 173.
2. For more on this topic see ibid.

If there is anything good, true, and beautiful in us, it is not an accident, but an intention. Other beings were also created, but only human beings were created with a unique role and privilege—that of being a reflection of the Creator Himself. From this comes human dignity. It is immense and unquantifiable, as our pre-modern fathers said.

This ontological determination of human beings was traditionally seen as the foundation of their moral purpose, that feeling of "oughtness." People somehow know or feel that they should live up to their calling. Not to act or behave beneath their dignity, "I should" follows from what I am. Ethics from ontology, humanity from humanness.

The anthropological intuition about the value of the human being has remained in our culture, even after its justification was removed by philosophy. Modernity programmatically rejected all metaphysics, and with it all ontology, yet most modern (and normal) people still insist that a human being has some real value. When a house is on fire, we save the people first, before the things.

The difference between the ontological and moral dimensions of human nature is clearly demonstrated in a meeting of the world of humans and the world of non-humans—no pejorative intended. Let us compare, for example, a brilliantly wicked man (such as Adolf Hitler) with any animal (such as a hamster). The fundamental question is, who is better? The answer is complex. It depends on what kind of good we're asking about: ontological or moral? Ontologically the man is obviously better, precisely because he is a person—he is endowed with unique potential, he is intelligent, charismatic, decisive, able to appreciate art, capable of great things. From this perspective we cannot even compare him to the hamster. Morally, on the other hand—if we can lend the hamster this category for a moment— the rodent is better because he is exactly what he should be: cute, hairy, and when he can, a hoarder. Exactly as his hamster-ness dictates. While Hitler—or anyone—if he commits a morally evil deed is acting against his humanity, that is, against his ontological nature.[3]

This brings us to the moral dimension of human nature, which is problematic, as I mentioned above. It's clear that there is something not right with people, or rather, with the moral capacity of human nature. Humans are not able to fulfill their moral calling. Yes, there is the moral imperative, that voice which says "I should"—but I don't listen to it, or I listen only selectively. To make things even more complicated, with a little

3. Cf. Kreeft, *Návrat*.

honest introspection I find that sometimes I downright don't want to listen, and take various steps to "mis-hear" it. Other times I hear it well and even want to obey, but cannot. "I shouldn't smoke so much." "I shouldn't take it." "I would never do that." And yet I find myself doing it again. I find that my will is (sometimes) good, but weak. I will return later to the question of the will. Now it is necessary to touch on the key question—isn't this all just fiction? Isn't this "voice of conscience" only a whip we artificially made ourselves? Isn't it only a construct—social, psychological or otherwise? The implication of such questions is obvious. If the answer is yes, then in the first place it has no objective validity, and therefore cannot make any claim on me—and in the second place we can freely manipulate it, reconstruct it, or completely deconstruct it. I am afraid that this is the core of our current problem, and it is also the reason we have to reintroduce ethical education into our schools. Along with Hobbes, Darwin, Freud, and Nietzsche, we first stripped human beings of their dignity ("we are nothing more than . . ."), and then also of their ethics ("we don't have to do more than . . ."). And now we do not know what to do with a morally illiterate generation.[4]

As I hinted at in the introduction, I am convinced that things are different with us in our humanity and our humanness. Our dignity is not a fiction or a construct. It is real. And therefore our moral calling is also real. However much our conscience can be burdened by pathological demands which are heaped upon it by our environment (in the sense of Freud's superego), it is also true that in many respects the demands of conscience are completely healthy, legitimate and real. That is, what they are asking for is truly good (or bad), not good "for me" or good "for the powerful majority" or "for a special interest group," or even "for a given culture," but good in its objective essence, good for the humanity of a person. People have mutually agreed on traffic rules as well as table manners, and if it's necessary they can be changed at any time. However, the rules of humanity are not liable to subjective preferences or social contract, nor can they be voted on or negotiated. Treachery, cowardice, and arrogance will always be immoral, even if most people or even a whole culture votes that they want it otherwise.[5]

4. Cf. Sokol, *Etika*.

5. I express this with the full knowledge that some of the current politically correct ideology of multiculturalism forbids its devotees to criticize any other culture, on the grounds that they are all of equal value. I don't agree. Various cultures are of varying quality according to what values they allow to be cultivated (notice the root *cult*). The reader doesn't have to be a cultural anthropologist to see that different cultures are based on different ideological stances (cosmological, epistemological, anthropological, etc.),

A person can neither produce nor determine the laws of human morality. We can only recognize them, and accept them or not. It is similar to natural laws, observes Aristotle—a fire burns both in Greece and Persia.[6]

This non-subjectivity of ethics is made known to us in a variety of ways, often in common, everyday situations. For example, let's consider the situation of an ordinary quarrel or dispute. In such a situation we hear or utter statements like: "How would you like it if something like that was done to you?" "Not so fast!" "Aren't you going to share it with me?" "You should be ashamed of yourself!" "Don't tell!" "But you promised!" and so on.[7]

It's interesting that the one who utters such statements doesn't want to say only that the other's behavior bothers them, but they are referring to an objective standard of behavior whose knowledge is assumed by both. And this assumption is confirmed immediately, whether positively or negatively. The offender might be ashamed and try to fix things, or to explain their behavior, or to apologize. They may claim, for example, that it was necessary for some extraordinary reason, or they were justified in going too fast, or something happened that kept them from keeping their word, and so on. In every case it's clear that both parties are appealing to some law or criteria of decency, honesty, or morality which they both know. Although such an understanding tends to be "quiet," latent, without any complicated philosophical verbalization, it refers to a completely real reference point— a moral law which is valid for both, or everyone involved.[8] Without this reference point no moral discussion would be possible. People could fight like animals, but they could never quarrel in the human sense of the word. Quarrelling means that each one tries to show the other that they are wrong or in some way guilty of doing something they shouldn't have done. And it's not done from the perspective of one or the other's own framework of

---

and therefore qualitatively contain very different elements. See, for example, cultures containing completely unethical doctrines such as female circumcision, cannibalism, or Aryan purity.

6. See Aristotle, *Nicomachean Ethics*.

7. The following paragraphs are free paraphrases of the absolutely timeless *Radio Discussions* which C. S. Lewis conducted in 1943 for the BBC in order to encourage his fellow citizens during World War II. These, together with other broadcasts, were later published under the title *Mere Christianity* in 1981, and subsequently published in Czech in 1993 as *K jádru křesťanství*.

8. For a beautiful example of an intuitive experience of moral reality see Karel Čapek's story *The Scream* in the collection *Boží muka* [The Agony of God].

values, but from the perspective of morality as such. Something like this would be meaningless if there did not exist between the parties involved the criterion for distinguishing what is right and wrong. Just like it would make no sense to say that a football player fouled, if there were no established rules for playing football. And if there were no rules for playing, the game itself would not exist—or it would be a very dangerous game.[9]

From a certain point of view, the human language about good and evil is quite fascinating. We live in a universe which clearly contains entities such as good and evil. But even more astonishing is the fact that this universe also contains beings like us, who know about it. We have difficulty giving exact definitions of the concepts of good and evil, but we recognize their reality and the qualitative difference in their natures. C. S. Lewis expressed it well: "A man does not call a line crooked unless he has some idea of a straight line."[10] And elsewhere he adds "You can be good for the sake of goodness, you cannot be bad for the sake of badness. You can do a kind action for someone even when you are not feeling kind, only because to be kind is right; but no one ever did a cruel action simply because cruelty is wrong—but only because it was pleasant or useful to him. In other words, badness cannot succeed even in being bad in the same way in which goodness is good. Goodness is, so to speak, itself: badness is only spoiled goodness. And there must be something good first before it can be spoiled."[11]

There is one more observation that the reality of the moral law demonstrates very well. In addition to the persistent idea that we *should* behave in a certain way, there is also the fact that none of us actually does. Not that we would continually do only wrong things, I'm only saying that—in the words of C. S. Lewis—sometime "this year, or this month, or, more likely, this very day, we have failed to practice ourselves the kind of behavior we expect from other people."[12] In our defense we usually present various "extenuating circumstances" by which we have a tendency to somehow justify, excuse, or silence that relentless claim "you should/n't have done it." Such self-defense can take various forms: "I admit I behaved badly towards my wife, but I was so tired." "I had to cover up that questionable transaction or they would have fired me, and then how would I pay the mortgage?" "That thing I promised my neighbor I would do, but didn't, I never would

9. Schirrmacher, *Leadership*.

10. Lewis, *Mere Christianity*, 25.

11. Ibid., 28.

12. Ibid., 10.

have promised if I had known how much work I would have." It's not about whether or not the excuses are legitimate. The point is that the voice we hear within ourselves is real—it's our awareness of the moral law. It is part of being human: it's with me, in me, it's my conscience. If we didn't have one we would have no need of defending ourselves when we act against it, nor would we understand the concept of a "clean" conscience when we act in accordance with it.

The idea of a "clean" conscience of course, is notoriously problematic, because we humans possess an extraordinary range of psychological resources that allow us to keep a subjectively "clean" conscience, regardless of objective reality. Think about, for example, all the self-deceiving strategies such as rationalization, projection, suppression, cognitive dissonance, etc.[13] Many Eastern Europeans will remember the slogan that was popularly used to rationalize behavior under a totalitarian regime: "who doesn't steal from the government, steals from their family."[14] This, however, even further raises the need for an education in ethics which would teach how to relate to moral reality in the appropriate manner, that is, to cultivate the consciousness so that it would not "stray," as Anzenbacher puts it.[15]

It is worth mentioning one more moral-psychological moment with important social implications. The difficulty of the process of admission of guilt usually results in an interesting ethical disproportion—my moral lapses are always the fault of someone or something else; my morally good behavior, on the other hand, is always mine alone. This disproportion in certain circumstances might sometimes be viewed as cute or funny. But if it becomes a permanent feature of one's character it tends to become something quite tragic, complicating the life of the person as well as those around them—as anyone who has been forced to contend with a person with a long-term inability to admit their own guilt, knows very well. It is especially tragic when that weakness becomes typical for some socially-influential culture or subculture, like politics. Additionally, the more the sin is committed the stronger is the tendency to transfer blame. Therefore, one of the key components of a good ethical education is the refinement of such undesireable human tendencies.

13. Cf. Aronson, *Animal.*

14. For an example of a very successful strategy for "relieving" the conscience, see Freud's theory of the superego or Jung's theory of archetypes, where there is always some outside factor that is responsible for one's behavior, so the person is always off the hook.

15. Anzenbacher, *Úvod.* On the issue of conscience, see also Dacík, *Mravouka,* or Durkheim, *Moral Education.*

To recapitulate: a human being is an ambivalent being, ontologically good, not good morally. Yet in one's moral capacity a person is neither always, nor in everything, bad. We have wonderful potential at our disposal and we often use it as we should; but often, if not more often, we use it in a way we shouldn't, abusing it or not having a strong enough will to use it well. As far as the fundamental question of whether human beings are basically good, there is no simple or unequivocal answer. A simple answer in this case would necessarily be simplistic, because it would ignore some dimensions of human nature.

J. J. Rousseau, for example—if I can outline the main anthropological alternatives—didn't want to admit the moral depravity of the individual.[16] If we listen to him carefully we hear that a person is good both ontologically and morally. From birth. Rousseau romantically believed that if an individual has a chance to show themselves as good, they will take it. There is good there, don't spoil it, let it spontaneously—Rousseau liked to say, *naturally*—flourish. But there is a problem. If humans are entirely good, how can we explain their evil tendencies and actions? It's their surroundings, decaying culture, others, he says. Of course, the others are also people. And from birth they have received "good" as well as "bad" moral examples with which they have had to cope. When and how does good blossom? Rousseau is silent. But his romantic appeal lives on. I think that it's for two reasons. Firstly, it so easily excuses us. The idea that we are inherently good and everything is always someone or something else's fault (preferably nameless: "them" or "culture"), will always meet with a positive response. Another variation of the culprit is "genes" or "hormones," or other such determining factors. Secondly, Rousseau's anthropology makes life much easier for every teacher or educator. Education based on the assumption that children don't actually need to be educated is really attractive. The lofty rhetoric here legitimizes the inactivity of the teachers. All the liberal educators will love it. As well as those who are simply lazy.

At the other end of the anthropological spectrum we find the concept of a human being who is good neither ontologically nor morally. Among the first and most well known adherents of this concept were Nicollo Machiavelli and Thomas Hobbes, followed by many others. From their perspective we are basically animals, beasts; evolved, but still beasts. In his famous *Leviathan*, Hobbes described humankind as merely material beings, subject to material laws. From the beginning, a very loud voice resonates that human

16. See Rousseau, *Emil*.

beings are predetermined entities. They seek pleasure and avoid pain, especially the greatest pain of all, death. There is often someone standing in their way, a rival with whom they must fight to save their lives. Hobbes reminds us of the old saying, "A man is a wolf to another man."[17] All in all, human life is "nasty, brutish and short," he says elsewhere.[18] If a person is to survive, they must come to a (hypothetical) agreement: I won't devour you, you won't devour me, and we will both give up our freedom in favor of an overseer, who will make sure we stick to our agreement and punish those who don't. The overseer, or "sovereign," must have absolute power in order to tame the beasts. All totalitarian regimes and authoritarian pedagogies will love Hobbes. If Rousseau and all the other romantics advise no infringing on the natural development of the individual, Hobbes and his ilk demand intervention—shaping, machining, forcing, controlling, policing, punishing. For the one humans are entirely good, for the other they are entirely bad.

I am proposing another variation. An alternative which distinguishes the ontological-moral subtlety of human nature: in our being we are good, in our morality we are fallen. It is not a new or revolutionary anthropology, in fact it is so old and traditional it has become alternative. I believe that it both captures the state of "human affairs" authentically and realistically, and fundamentally defines how and what happens in an ethical education—as we shall see.

17. Hobbes quotes the Latin proverb "Homo hominis lupus est" in his *De Cive* (On the citizen). Available online: (1. 10. 2015), http://www.constitution.org/th/decive.htm.

18. Quotation from *Leviathan*, which is available in the original online, page 58 (1. 10. 2015), http://www.earlymoderntexts.com/assets/pdfs/hobbes1651part1_2.pdf#page=1&zoom=auto,-229,445.

Chapter 3

Is Everything Allowed?
A Note on the (Post)Modern Situation

Not long ago I spoke with a farmer from southwestern England. He was complaining that times are not what they used to be. He never imagined that he would have to lock his barn and garage. Things are being stolen as never before: crops, fertilizer, cattle, even tractors. The sociologists call this *the decline of social capital.*[1] People don't trust one another. The more stolen property, lying to clients, shoddy workmanship, broken promises and asset stripping of institutions, the less trust, the lower the capital. We are poorer. Despite the superabundance of material goods, we are suffering—we, advanced Western civilization—from increasing moral malnutrition. Things are still functioning in southwestern England, but in some places the situation is becoming critical. Interest in all levels of social life has moved from the margins of ethical themes to the forefront. In politics, economics, medicine, education, and virtually all areas of public life people are talking with a new intensity about the need for ethical principles, values and codes.[2] While ethics declines, the discussion about ethics grows, observes Peter Kreeft.[3] And the feverish discussion isn't coming from prudish moralists, but from the awareness of the "intersubjective dependency" of one person

---

1. Cf. Sedláčková, *Důvěra.*

2. See the huge amount of recent literature on this theme. For example, Honneth, *Sociální*; Sutor, *Politická*; Haškovcová, *Lékařská*; Furger, *Etika*; Chapman, *Etika*; Johnson, *Christian Ethics*; Nullens and Michener, *Matrix.*

3. Kreeft, *Návrat.*

with another, without which we cannot safely share a common world.[4] The stakes are the very "ethical habitability of the globe," which for the first time in its history is being threatened by its own inhabitants.[5] Gilles Lipovetsky even warns that "the twenty-first century will be ethical, or it will not be at all."[6] The ethical deficit which current society is feeling is calling forth a "new demand for virtuous people."[7]

How did we get here? Are people today more corrupt and morally fallen than those of previous generations? I don't think so. Anthropologically speaking, the essence of our humanity hasn't changed; what has changed is the environment and scope in which the ethical potential of our humanity is realized, or developed—whether towards authentic humanity or degenerating into inhumanity. Our modern philosophical arena, which we have crowned with critical epithets such as post-modern, hyper-modern, super-modern and the like, is related to the sense of a crisis of modernity and the specific ways it forms our ethical thinking and behavior. What, then, is our "modern" postmodernity?[8]

The paradox is that when the story of modernity was born, it looked very promising for ethics. The slogan of the Enlightenment was *sapere aude*, encouraging people to "have the courage to think independently." It was a (quite understandable) reaction to the medieval tradition of reliance on external authority. The Enlightenment understood itself as the age of adolescence for humanity, as the great moment in history when humanity finally summoned the courage to liberate itself from the clutches of ignorance. And the instrument of emancipation became the newly discovered human *ratio* (reason), by which one could hope to "to uncover, describe and explain the entire natural order of things," and do it completely autonomously.[9]

In addition to a belief in the almost omnipotent ability of reason, the script of the modern story was also built on a belief in the moral progress

4. Lorenzová, *O smyslu*.

5. Cf. Kohák, *Člověk*; Kreeft, *Choices*.

6. Lipovetsky, *Soumrak*, 11.

7. Sokol and Pinc, *Antropologie*. Cf. MacIntyre, *After Virtue*; Kilpatrick, *Moral Illiteracy*; Lickona, *Educating*.

8. The allusion to the work of Wolfgang Welsch (*Naše postmoderní*) is intentional, because I identify with Welsch's understanding of postmodernity as an extension of modernity.

9. Wright, *Religion*. I will base my description of modernity here primarily on Wright's text, because I find his metanarrative very relevant to issues of ethics and ethical education, which I will deal with later.

of humanity. Stanley Grenz expressed it well: "The modern scientist considers it axiomatic that what knowledge discovers, is always good. This assumption of the intrinsic goodness of knowledge made the enlightened worldview optimistic. It led to the belief that progress is inevitable, that science together with the power of education will eventually free us from all vulnerability to nature and all social slavery."[10] Encouraged by the developments in the field of science, modern humanity began to believe in progress in the field of morality. For the one who "rightly" knows, will likewise "rightly" act. The question of the relationship between *scientia* a *conscientia* was not in itself anything new, but the assumption that science and education will automatically be humanizing factors in the process of ennobling human beings got its doctrinal form only within the framework of the modern story. Modernity believed that the upward progress of humanity towards a better future is inevitable and that it is only a question of time, when, thanks to the unstoppable expansion of knowledge, we will be able to control the natural world, even "command the wind and the rain," until at last we reach the coveted paradise on earth.[11]

According to Andrew Wright, the optimistic faith of the Enlightenment led to the emergence of three interconnected metanarratives,[12] which together constitute the essence of modernity.

The Naturalistic Metanarrative of the hegemony of science, providing technical control over the physical world. The naturalistic concept of the world was (and often still is) based on the epistemological assumption that one can maintain a non-problematic distance from the object under study (the world). The newly discovered "omnipotence" of human reason fostered the establishment of the certainty of knowledge as a means of linking rationality with the natural order of things. These efforts presupposed the so-called *correspondence theory of truth*, based on the harmony between human thought and external reality. Wright demonstrated that the distinction between the internal operations of the mind and the external reality of the physical world had its roots in Descartes's identification of "mental" and "physical" as the two essential substances, or basic building blocks, of

10. Grenz, *Primer*, 14.

11. I discuss the specific pedagogical implications arising from the progressive optimism of the modern paradigm elsewhere. See Hábl, *Human Goals*.

12. The term "metanarrative" is taken from Jean-Francois Lyotard, *The Postmodern Condition*. Lyotard defined it as the great, all-encompassing story of a society which explains its meaning. The postmodern era is characterized by Lyotard as one of disbelief in meta-stories.

the universe.[13] In this view the role of language is to create a bridge between the mental and the physical, that the mind would be the mirror of external reality, its exact representation. The role of experience is indispensable here—it forms the basis of all knowing. There is nothing in the mind that was not first in the senses. By exactly describing empirical experience one is able to achieve real certainty about the natural world. Millard J. Erickson states that this epistemic optimism is founded on the presupposition that the structure of reality is rational:

> The structure of reality is rational. It follows an orderly pattern. The same logical structure of the external world is also found in the human mind, thus enabling the human to know and organize that world. In most cases, this order or pattern is believed to be immanent within the world, rather than deriving from some transcendent source.[14]

Stephen Toulmin describes this aspect of thought as a typical modern "policy of certainty" recalling the socio-political dimension of the whole phenomenon. The desire for certain (sure) knowledge was not only an exercise for academics, but it was also a "timely response to a particular historical challenge: the political, social, and theological chaos expressed, among other things, by the Thirty Years' War."[15]

Modern thinkers, however, were not deaf to Descartes's concerns about the reliability of the senses. While David Hume represented the skeptical line of empirical philosophy, the logical positivists stood on the other side of the philosophical spectrum. With their verification principle of testing all truthful statements by empirical experience they sought to overcome Hume's skepticism. Wright observed the implications of positivism:

> This [principle of verification] effectively reduces all moral, aesthetic and religious discourse to the level of emotive utterances incapable of engaging cognitively with the real world; it is not possible to verify on the basis of sense experience whether a person is good, a sunset beautiful, or God holy, since we can neither see, smell, taste, touch or hear goodness, beauty or holiness.[16]

---

13. Wright, *Religion*, 16.

14. Erickson, *Truth*, 74.

15. Toulmin, *Cosmopolis*, 71.

16. Wright, *Religion*, 17.

The practical consequences of the hegemony of naturalistic metanarratives are two, according to Wright: "reality is reduced to a morally valueless (because) deterministic game of the causes and effects of the physical world; the scientist is promoted to the position of arbiter, mediator, and high priest of ultimate truth."[17]

The second metanarrative of modernity carries the attribute *Romantic*. It is an idealistic alternative to the preceding narrative, related to the search for sense or meaning. According to the idealists, our understanding of the meaning of things as well as of life itself does not have its roots in sensory experience, but rather in mental ideas, pictures, and constructions present in the mind of the person. Francis A. Schaeffer writes that this romantic reaction was motivated by the increasing pressure of naturalistic determinism—"as man (sic) begins to feel the weight of the machine pressing upon him (sic), Rousseau and others swear and curse, as it were, against the science which threatens their human freedom.[18]

In place of the Correspondence Theory of Truth—to describe the order of reality—the romantics made do with a mere *Coherence Theory*, according to which the truth of any system of statements is judged by their internal coherency and interconnectedness. The work of language here "is not to build a bridge between the mind and the external world, but rather to give coherent expression to our inner thoughts, experiences, and intuitions."[19]

Classical examples of modern idealism can be found in the grand philosophic systems developed by Spinoza, Leibnitz, and Hegel, for example, and an embryonic version can be traced back to Immanuel Kant. Kant distinguished "noumena" from "phenomena," that is, reality as it is in itself from reality as it appears to human beings, which led to a fundamental shift in philosophic discourse. According to Kant, human understanding of reality depends on the innate structures of the mind through which we perceive reality. As a result, we only have access to the phenomenological world of appearances, but never the noumenal world of things as they are in themselves. "Following Kant," commented Wright, "I can no longer say

17. Ibid., 18.

18. Schaeffer, *How Should We*, 228. It is necessary, however, to explain that the mechanistic concept of human beings and nature was not originally considered to be negative. Charles van Doren (*History*, 214–16) quotes Adam Smith (1723–1790), who marveled at the fascinating association of human and non-human elements in factory machinery, which he saw as a potential source of "universal wealth" for the whole world.

19. Wright, *Religion*, 19.

'This is the case', only that 'It appears to me that this is the case.' Kant thus unwittingly gave birth to a distinctively modern mode of expression: 'From my point of view . . .', 'The way I see it . . .', 'In my opinion . . . .'"[20]

Thus the romantic metanarrative, together with Descartes's emphasis on reflexive introspection, produced a particular freedom to "read" reality according to one's own subjective referential framework. "Nobody has the right to tell me that my experience is illegitimate, my reasoning incorrect, or my emotions misdirected. Hence the truth of my value system lies not in its connection with any external order, nor in any objective or ontological foundation, but simply in the fact that I have an emotional commitment to it."[21]

The third metanarrative of modernity is founded on the *liberal imperative of freedom and tolerance*, through which cultural diversity is guarded and adjusted. The naturalistic and romantic efforts in the quest for certain knowledge and the true meaning of life caused a tension which called for resolution. "In attempting to reconcile the realms of fact and value," said Wright, "modernity forged a third, unifying metanarrative: liberalism, which sought to mediate between naturalism and romanticism by establishing a framework within which they could learn to live together in relative harmony *despite* their significant differences."[22] The resulting liberal polity was built on the twin principles of freedom of belief, and tolerance of the beliefs of others.

The roots of liberalism can be traced back to John Locke.[23] He was able, relatively early, to recognize the practical limits of naturalism—we all hold some beliefs which are subjective in nature: the limits of human knowledge are so narrow and the probability of error on speculative matters so great that we can never know for certain that our religious opinions are correct and all others false and heretical," said Wright.[24] Thus Locke constituted the principle of freedom in all matters that could not be shown to establish indisputable and incorrigible factual knowledge.

20. Kant, *O výchově*, 19.

21. Wright, *Religion*, 20.

22. Ibid., 21.

23. Greer and Lewis, *History*, connected the origin of the liberal meta-story with even older thinkers such as, for example, Erasmus and Rabelais. Like Wright, they affirmed that "the central theme of these men was their emphasis on the personhood of a human being and one's free development. They believed it could only be realized if each individual would exercise their personal freedom."

24. Wright, *Religion*, 21.

In time, that liberal strategy satisfied both camps. The naturalists could devote themselves to the safe results of scientific research, the romantics could uninterruptedly make use of their subjective morals and aesthetics or spiritual experiences. The cost of this liberal arrangement was relatively acceptable. All we had to do was submit to the imperative of tolerance. If I want the right to think and believe what I want, I have to be willing to respect the right of others to do the same.

Wright noted that although the motif was originally heuristic, it gradually turned into a narrowly dogmatic worldview. As soon as the liberal principles became the ends in themselves, adherence to them began to be strictly monitored and enforced. In this way, the Enlightenment ideal of courage for independent thought was recast as the liberal ideal of "individuals thinking for themselves within the confines and constraints of the non-negotiable liberal order."[25]

Naturally, the spirit of modernity soon found its reflection in ethics and moral education. In the purely ethical sphere Kant's contribution is widely known: autonomous reason makes the moral imperative clear, without the need for metaphysical justification. An example of moral education can be seen in the equally well known approach of Emil Durkheim. His *L'éducation morale*, as well as others of his works, form a unique example of modern rationalism applied both from the point of view of education, and from the point of view of the newly emerging field of sociology. Durkheim, with complete confidence, assumes that morals anchored in metaphysics are passé, and seeks to replace them with a new "lay" authority which would respond to the changes and needs of modern society. Here he discovers (in simplified terminology) *social entity*—that particular phenomenon and space where the consciousness of the collective meets with that of the individual and both together dynamically form human convictions, attitudes, rules, norms, and so on.[26] The presumption of humanistic anthropocentrism is a matter of course in Durkheim's system, as indicated in the following words: "Such a morality, that is, the lay morality of the cult of the individual, is not merely some hygenic discipline or shrewd economics of existence; it is a religion in which the person is both believer and God," interprets M. Strouhal.[27]

25. Ibid., 22.
26. Cf. Durkheim, *Moral Education*.
27. Strouhal, *Několik poznámek*.

Under the assumption that there really is nothing which could invincibly defy human reason, and that the real world in which we live and the ideal world which we have to bring to fruition are both grasped by means of the same scientific tools, Durkheim applies the epistemological and methodological principles of the social sciences to the areas of morality and pedagogy.[28] From his analysis it follows that moral behavior comprises its own, internal authority, and as such, is not dissimilar to Kant's categorical imperative. However Durkheim does not derive it metaphysically, but sociologically. It's necessary to properly present, explain, and justify this authoritative entity to learners. Durkheim says "explain," not "preach," because moral principles must be "freely desired and received," and that free reception is nothing other than an acceptance of the clarification.[29] Only then—Durkheim believes—will the individual have "true moral knowledge and education." In short, in Durkheim's conception it is never possible to understand the educational impact as socialization by morality, but as moralization by sociality, as Strouhal aptly put it. Durkheim believes that "sociality" (the social entity) will function as an authoritative background for the desired "cultivation of the person and the development of the seeds of humanity that are in us."[30]

The question is whether Durkheim's "sociality" is able to guarantee the legitimacy of moral conduct and educational activity. It seems that Durkheim himself recognized this problem and therefore spoke of the necessity of preserving the "sanctity" of his new anti-metaphysical authority, which would guarantee his "lay" morality. Strouhal observes that this is the biggest difficulty with Durkheim's concept of moral education—the lack of a meta-ethical anchor; in Strouhal's words he cannot "show, substantiate or internalize in children the necessity of fulfilling the duties and obligations which are the very heart of morality."[31]

The hopeful outlook for modernity began to slowly fall apart during the twentieth century. It turned out that even though science brings unprecedented technical possibilities, by itself it cannot ensure humanity and moral refinement. It is clearly true that the one who knows, has power, as Francis Bacon noted.[32] Likewise it is without dispute that one must be led

---

28. Cf. Durheim, *Sociologie*; Strouhal, *K morálním*.

29. Strouhal, *K morálním*.

30. Ibid.

31. Ibid.

32. Bacon repeated many times the idea that *scientia potentia est* (knowledge is

to knowledge, that is, educated. However, historical experience has shown that knowledge and education can be used for good as well as for evil. In light of the attrocities of the twentieth century in which science actively participated, the modern assumption of automatic humanity seems ridiculous, if not reprehensibly naive. Through science we have tremendous power, but we have no control over this power. In the second half of the twentieth century, instead of gratefully giving themselves into the care of the scientists, people gradually began to develop a cautious mistrust. People tended to watch the scientists with increasing suspicion and apprehension—who knew what kind of abuse their techno-scientific creations could be used for?[33] Moreover, the extraordinary developments in technology and science, which have given Western society unprecedented power and prosperity, have also produced a number of problems which have grown to global proportions, and with which nobody knows what to do. The culture of surplus and prosperity contrasts sharply with the miserable reality of millions of starving, destitute, illiterate, and marginalized individuals and entire nations, which the "civilized" world does not know how to help because it has so many problems of its own. Its advanced technocracy has generated a series of anti-humane manifestations such as the objectification of the human being, the alienation of the individual, the impersonalization of human relationships, etc. Instead of the long-awaited paradise on earth, sociologists warn of a dramatic decline in moral literacy, a fall in social capital, threats of global self-destruction, clashes of civilizations, various forms of extremism, and the like. The accounts of the migrants to the West are telling—we want your prosperity but we don't want your morality.

Another problem with the modern meta-story which contributed to its collapse was its tendency towards totalitarianism, that is, to make itself the exclusive interpreter of reality and a tool of power. Michel Foucault described it well when he noted how modern scientific discourse has been used as a means for all-pervasive dominance and supervision.[34] The form of totalitarian power can change, but its essence remains the same. In this way, under the auspices of the great stories several totalitarian attrocities were legitimized—from the colonialization of the West[35] to Communisim in the

---

power) in his timely revolutionary reflections, which particularly inspired even our Comenius. See, e.g., Bacon, *Nové organon*, 89, 186.

33. Cf. Bauman, *Individualizovaná*, 159.

34. Foucault, *Dohlížet*.

35. In this contex Finkielkraut nicely puts his finger on the link between the concepts

East[36] to the so-called neo-liberal pragmatism which appears to flourish in every corner of the earth.[37]

As a result, all the safe reference points and formulas that make the modern world function reliably, and which facilitate the choosing of meaningful life strategies, have faded away. The coming generation, weaned on postmodern milk, no longer knows reality as a cohesive whole in which it's possible to find meaning and logic, but rather as a hodge-podge of random and uncertain events. They don't believe in any "great story," grand ideas, all-encompassing explanations of the world, or the institutions which represent them. Nor do they believe that any kind of scientific, business, economic, or even political measures can secure a better existence than their parents had. For the "post-factual generation,"[38] truth is an empty concept that means whatever anyone wants it to mean. Objective knowledge is irrelevant. The law and justice are left to the mercy of interpretation. Polititians do not have to be truthful to win the elections, they need to be impressive. The advancement of humanity is a long-lost romantic illusion. Moral principles are thoroughly relativized. Everything is permissible.[39]

We find that we cannot live well in such a world. With every extra billion stolen from the state budget, with every further broken promise, with every word not held to, or deceptive advertisement, the people's moral nausea for a system which they must adapt to, grows.[40] Hence the call for ethics and an education in ethics in our schools. It is almost certain that no book, lecture, or article on ethics will make people behave more virtuously. But one thing is sure—we need an education in ethics. And that, to

---

of colonization and civilization when he says that for the modern West, civilization meant "making one's current conditions a pattern, one's own habits a universal power, one's values the absolute criteria for judging, and the European man the master and owner of nature, the most interesting being in creation . . . Because Europe embodied progress for other societies, colonization seemed seemed to be the fastest, most noble means for bringing lagging societies onto the track of civilization. Developed nations saw their mission: to speed up the path for non-Europeans to education and prosperity. It was necessary, for the good of the primitive nations, to absorb their differences—that is, their backwardness—into the Western universality" (Destrukce, 42).

36. Everyone who has lived under a Communist regime knows the concrete consequences of the totalitarian discourse, which has its grand story about the class struggle and which—don't forget—should eschatalogically end in the promised paradise on earth.

37. Bělohradský, Společnost.

38. Lorenzová, O smyslu.

39. Kreeft, Návrat; Johnson, Christian Ethics.

40. Compare Bělohradský's "nausea" in his Společnost nevolnosti.

summarize, is for the three reasons which I have tried to outline so far. First of all, morality, or ethics, are fundamentally embedded in our human nature and from birth we are able to become moral beings, possessing a moral potential which literally calls for its actualization. Secondly, there is an objective ethical reality which has a claim on us. And thirdly—we all know from experience that without ethical boundaries and brakes we are threatened with self-destruction.

Chapter 4

What Kind of Ethics to Teach?

THE QUESTION I RAISE in the title of this chapter needs a certain specification. I am not going to deal with various theories such as deontological ethics, pragmatic ethics, the ethics of virtue, or the like, nor will I explain individual methodological approaches like descriptive, normative, or applied ethics. This chapter is about the three basic dimensions contained in every kind of ethics, or with which they all somehow deal. They are the individual, social, and meta-ethical aspects.

I present these three aspects together, because current ethico-educational discourse tends to emphasize only one of them, as suggested by the frequency of the use of the term *pro-sociality* in current literature.[1] In light of the "state of morals" and "ill health of individualism" it is necessary to first cultivate the kind of behavior that "would benefit another or a group of others."[2] Likewise, the individual themes which form the curriculum of various approaches to ethical education are determined for their (pro)social emphases, for example a positive evaluation of others, empathy, appropriate assertiveness, communication, solidarity, and the like. Pro-sociality also stipulates the methodological principles of educational style, where trust plays the key role between teacher and student, unconditional acceptance,

---

1. I will discuss this interesting neologism later. Occasionally *pro-social and ethical* terms are used as if they have equivalent meanings. See, e.g., Podolská, *Prosociální*. For the concept of *pro-socialism* see also the official pages of the Ethical Forum of the Czech Republic at http://www.etickeforumcr.cz, or Švarcová, *Možnosti etické*; Collected authors, *Na cestě*; Vacek, *Rozvoj*.

2. Podolská, *Prosociální*, 2.

positive reinforcement, and so on.[3] All of these pro-social efforts are un-doubtedly good, needed, even necessary, especially in the context of the dramatic decline of the aforementioned social capital, when people stopped believing other people.[4]

However, it is also necessary to state that the individual and meta-ethical dimensions of ethics are just as important as the social ones. The problem will be best explained by an illustration.[5] Imagine humanity as a naval fleet which is setting sail on a mission. If the ships are to accomplish their task they must fulfill three basic conditions. First, each individual ship must be seaworthy. Second, every ship must sail without crossing any other ship's path, they must not bump into each other or shoot a gun or torpedo at another of them. And third, the entire fleet must know where and why they are sailing. The point is obvious. If there are constant clashes between the ships they will never reach their goal. But it is also true that if the rudders don't work properly they won't be able to avoid a crash. Likewise, they must help each other to accomplish their mission. Nevertheless, even if the fleet were able to sail relatively free from conflict (which is nearly impossible in real life), it would fail in its mission if the fleet did not know the goal of its enterprise. In short—ethics deals with all three of the areas mentioned. We could call the first the internal health of the individual, or functional conscience, or individual ethics. The second area deals with relationships, harmony, and coexistence among individuals, or social ethics. The third concerns the meaning of behavior as a whole, the goal towards which the entire fleet is directed, or meta-ethics.[6]

The aim of this chapter is to present the following argument—all three of these aspects of ethics are mutually inseparable. Part of the argument is the assumption that a person is not only "homo prosocialis," but that hu-manity comes to fruition on all three of these levels. The point of applying

3. Compare the Úvodem of Ladislav Lencz to the *Etické výchově* of Roche-Olivar.

4. This issue has been addressed from various points of view by several authors. See, for example, Bauman, *Individualizovaná*; Lipovetsky, *Soumrak*; Fuchs, *Naše jednání*; Kreeft, *Choices*; Kohák, *Člověk*.

5. The following illustration and its application for the individual part of ethics is paraphrased from Lewis, *Mere Christianity*.

6. The term "meta-ethics" is used here in its traditional sense. The reader should be warned however, that relatively recent this term has begun to be used in another sense. Under the influence of some of Witgenstein's works a new trend has emerged in ethical thinking: it examines the language we use to make ethical statements and tries to determine their meaningfulness. Because it is a certain (linguistic) meta-discourse, it too is being called meta-ethics, which could be confusing to the lay reader.

the argument to education is that if ethics is to be functional, it must cultivate humanity in all of its moral complexity, that is, it must be cultivated as
much in the individual and meta-ethical dimensions as in the social.

The current emphasis on the social dimension of ethics is, to a large
extent, understandable. On the one hand the consequences of bad social
morality are the most visible, and on the other hand they put the greatest burden on us (society). Every instance of corruption, public lying,
fraudulent work, stolen billions, or war unleashed are chiefly social problems requiring urgent resolution. It is therefore no wonder that the individual morality of each of us is overshadowed or allocated to purely private
spheres.[7] In private everyone is allowed to do what they want, especially
if they are decent, respectable, hard-working citizens. An example of such
thinking could be the case of a politician or other socially well-known person who does something unethical in their personal life (for example, a famous politician is caught in adultery). If the prevailing ethical tendency of
society is an emphasis on individual morality or categorical accountability
to meta-ethical authority, then such behavior would be socially unacceptable. Because, however, the tendency to not solve the great meta-questions
predominates and in the name of "tolerance" no one infringes on anyone's
privacy, the politician remains in his or her position, unthreatened. Then
this becomes seen as normal and harmless behavior, and gradually is trans-
formed into the moral standard and pattern.

A similar logic can be seen in statements of the type "as long as it
doesn't hurt anyone, it's okay," where the determining criteria for whether
the behavior is good or bad is again a social one. Going back to our illustration, then, the one who thinks this way would say that it doesn't matter
what happens inside the ship, as long as it doesn't hurt anyone.

But it would be a mistake, and a crucial one, to implement this thinking into ethical education because it would fundamentally reduce, if not
completely destroy, its effectiveness. What would be the good of explaining
how to steer a ship so as to avoid a crash if the ship itself is such a wretched,
leaky wreck that it can't be steered at all? What is the purpose of contriving
or instilling social rules of behavior and coexistence, if we know that our
cowardice, greed, envy, indifference, or conceit will prevent us from following them? Of course, this doesn't mean that we shouldn't think about
improving and developing our social system. We must think hard, clarify
laws, make regulations, and amend the rules. But all these efforts would

7. Cf. Bauman, *Individualizovaná*; Lipovetsky, *Soumrak*.

be futile if we overlooked the fact that not even the best law or system will function properly without (in this case morally) functioning individuals. For example, it is relatively easy to set up a system of conditions to eliminate corruption, license and other social discord—every time an instance of it appears we deal with it legislatively, we forbid it. But as long as there are still devious shysters (immoral individuals), they will always find a way to play the same old game in every new system.[8] In other words, "you cannot make men good by law, and without good men you cannot have a good society."[9] Therefore the pedagogical cultivation of ethics is necessary, not only (pro)socially, but also individually.[10]

As has been mentioned, in addition to the social and individual levels there is also the level of meta-ethics.[11] The meta-ethical questions are not so much specific questions about what is good in this or that case, but rather fundamental questions of the type: What is good? What does it mean to live a good life?

Even though the questions are difficult we cannot ignore them, because meta-ethical pre-understanding necessarily precedes ethical practice. Earlier, in the Introduction, I explained that everyone has some kind of pre-understanding, whether it is reflected or not, of good quality or poor quality, consistent or contradictory, or even whether it is faulty.[12] Different meta-ethical starting points, of course, result in different—often radically different—ethical behaviors. Consider the difference between two systems

8. For example, we can legislatively control the amount of emissions a vehicle can send into the air, but an ethically uncultivated individual or group of individuals will think up a way to circumvent that law; for specific examples see articles in any news periodical, such as <http://www.reflex.cz/clanek/zpravy/66536/strucne-a-jednoduse-jak-a-proc-volkswagen-podvadel-s-emisemi.html> Available online (29. 9. 2015).

9. Lewis, *Mere Christianity*, 43.

10. The discussion on concrete ways of shaping individual character goes beyond the scope of this work, but it is clear that it isn't merely some kind of "painless" practice of certain patterns of behavior or social competence. The building of individual virtue is a relatively demanding, complex and long-term affair requiring considerable effort of the part of educator and student. Consider, for example, what it takes and how long it takes for a natural tendency towards selfishness and laziness to turn into a tendency towards self-sacrifice and hard work.

11. For further information on meta-ethics see Kolář and Svoboda, *Logika*; Holmes, *Ethics*.

12. The attribute "wrong" sounds like pure blasphemy to the confirmed ethical relativist. Nevertheless, I use it because I am convinced that not all factors of good ethics are relative. To the question "What is good?" it is possible to find the true answer, but it's also possible to be wrong. If it were not so, any discussion about ethics would be pointless.

of thought when one presumes absolute autonomy of the individual, while the other does not. Or let us return once more to our naval illustration. Those individuals whose morality is determined only by their relationships to others know that they should not damage the other ships in the fleet, however they are also unwaveringly convinced that it is no one's business what they do in or with their own ship. But isn't the crucial difference that of whether the person is the owner of the ship or just the captain who is responsible to the real owner? In plain English, isn't it crucial what a person thinks or who they believe regarding the true meaning of their life—to whom they ultimately have to answer? There is a difference if a person is answerable only to themself versus to an outside authority—therefore I believe that it is not possible to neglect or ignore the meta-ethical level. On the contrary, it is necessary to ponder it, rectify it, refine it, and at the same time examine its integrity in relation to specific ethical behavior.

The negative consequences of neglecting the meta-ethical dimension are especially evident in education. No matter how didactically sophisticated we appear, if we never talk about a meta-ethical basis for our actions then sooner or later we are perceived as merely moralizing. The demand "be good, son" can be raised in various pedagogical ways—authoritarian or nonviolently, amusingly, painlessly. In any case the child in time will grow up and want to know *why*. Why is this or that good or evil? Why are they laying moral expectations on me?

The problem for teachers of ethics is that our current (apparently still postmodern) culture does not go in for the great "why" questions. In this respect, postmodernity is really an extension of modernity, which said goodby to metaphysics from the time of Rousseau, Kant, and Durkheim. However, without a meta-authority the educator has nothing with which to legitimize a specific ethical imperative. If children or students ask why they should be good, they get only non-meta-ethical responses which are hardly satisfactory. For example, a psychologizing answer would offer something like—because good behavior is our natural psychological need and brings us satisfaction. The student's response to that is—if you only knew what would bring me satisfaction . . . I have no reason to act according to your idea of what is good. Or a utilitarian answer to the question of why a student should be good might be—because it's useful, or expedient. And the student's comeback—expedient for you maybe, but not for me.[13]

13. The shift in ethical trends can easily be seen in the everyday reality of our current world. For example, in the IKEA restaurants a customer can read the following on the wall: "Why it is good to clean up your own dishes. Leaving a clean table at IKEA is one of

A supporter of the social contract theory would say—because the majority of us have agreed on it. The individualist student who wants to sail his own ship autonomously rejects that answer with a response like—so let's make a different agreement. In other words, neither psychological, pragmatic, social, nor any other reasons have the meta-ethical potential to justify morality as such. The answers are similar to those in the children's story *Why is the Ocean Salty?* It's salty because it's salty. Why should I be good? Because it's good to do that. If a teacher is unable to give better—non-tautological—answers, ethical education can't function. However playful, entertaining, non-directive or user-friendly they may be, the absence of a meta-ethical anchor leaves the ethical imperatives in the philosophical air. And children are ususally very perceptive philosophers.

The restrictions on metaphysics and meta-ethics are understandable from the historical and philosophical points of view. "Why" questions have always been notoriously contentious. Which meta-instance is the "right one"? Who says what is good and what is bad? Zeus? Višna? The Lord? Allah? Or maybe Jehovah? It might not be so hard to distinguish, but we fear ideologizing, radicalizing, and sectarianism, especially in schools. Therefore, we give over or assign the meta questions to the ideological-private sphere—sail your own boat, believe what you want, just don't hurt me. And above all—don't ask where we're going. This has been working for a long time. But we're beginning to realize that the fleet is unsustainable. Civilization is morally drowning.

"The twenty-first century will either be ethical, or it won't be at all," warned Lipovetsky, as I mentioned in the Introduction.[14] Several paragraphs will be devoted to his contribution to the discussion, because it is an excellent example of ethics without meta-ethics. The quotation is from his book *The Twilight of Duty*, with the subtitle *The Painless Ethics of the New Democratic Times* [Le crépuscule du devoir. L'éthique indolore des nouveaux temps démocratiques]. The sociologizing style here exemplifies the postmoralist attitude of the present which doesn't hold to the great "imperatives or transcendental moral brakes" that there used to be in the

---

the reasons you pay less! When you put your own tray and dishes in the container we can keep our prices lower. Our employees will have more time to prepare and serve food." It is worth noting how the argument is constructed—it doesn't appeal to any meta-authority, it doesn't assume any categorical imperative of the type "cleaning up after yourself is decent," it doesn't invoke the good that is somehow within each of us. It tries to convince the customer that it is advantageous. Utilitarianism in practice.

14. Lipovetsky, *Soumrak*, 11.

past when duty was sacred, or rationally categorical. "Let's not deceive ourselves," urged Lipovetsky, "whatever commotion there currently is around ethics, the dynamics of rejection and euphemization of duty continues on its way ... What kind of attention is given to moral instructions in a society which is obsessed with youth and health? . . . Happiness or nothing." And elsewhere he adds, "The ambition of the moralistic age was to discipline desire, we stimulate it; the moralist era encouraged adherence to certain obligations to ourselves and others, we worship comfort. Temptation has replaced obligation, prosperity has become our god and advertising is his prophet."[15] Lipovetsky furnishes such ethics with the appropriate attribute *painless* and explains that it doesn't demand renunciation, self-denial, sacrifice or disciplining of individual desires. He calls this kind of ethics "minimal" or "the third type." He claims that it does not rule out one's right to individual self-realization, happiness, comfort or personal freedom.[16]

The preliminary question then, is whether such an ethics offers any kind of potential to resolve the ethical problems of our time. Or to put it another way, whether such an "ethics" is ethical. Lipovetsky believes it is. He admits that although it isn't very "noble," nevertheless it is apparently "better adapted to a technical, democratic society," and as such is certainly "more suited to coping with the great risks of the future."[17] Where is its potential? Lipovetsky thinks it's in "the effort to reconcile values and interests, to merge the rights of the individual with the restrictions imposed by society, economics and science . . . [the effort] to balance the expansion of individualistic logic with the legitimization of new collective obligations; it is in a fair compromise between today and tomorrow, prosperity and preservation of the environment, scientific advancement and humanism."[18] In other words—the pragmatic necessity for survival will teach us to play ethically. "Therefore, let's not call for ethical heroism," concludes Lipovetsky, "but [call for] social development of *intelligent ethics* . . . which seeks to find the just center or equitable peace with regard to the historical, technical and social circumstances."[19] The attribute "intelligent" is elsewhere rounded out

15. Ibid., 61–62.
16. Cf. ibid., 59.
17. Ibid., 237.
18. Ibid., 232.
19. Ibid., 238.

with further terms such as "responsible," "reasonable," "dialogical," and "humanistic."[20]

Lipovetsky is an excellent observer, his description of the context of current postmoralistic ethics is first-rate, and his identification of such an ethics as painless and without obligation is accurate. Lipovetsky is also aware of the need to find a compromising solution between the rights and requirements of the individual on the one hand, and collective commitments on the other—his proposal therefore expects some form of individual and social ethics. But where is the meta-ethical dimension? The author makes no mention of it at all, he only states that all the transcendental "brakes" used in the past to, in some way, both diminish immorality and encourage moral heroism, are now passé. Nevertheless, he hopes to "negotiate" such an ethics which—despite being painless and without obligation—will have qualities and attributes such as "responsible, reasonable, intelligent, dialogical, and humanistic." The fundamental question must be asked—how are these qualities to be achieved without the renunciation, self-denial, sacrifice, and restraining of individual tendencies? The author does not respond. "Balance, equitable peace, a sense of responsibility" and so on must be sought, but it must not require any effort or pain. We need ethics, but don't ask me for an ethical exertion. We need a considerate society, but don't make me deny myself.

The problem with Lipovetsky's ethics can be see even more clearly in a pedagogical application. Is it possible to educate someone towards responsibility or justice without self-denial or self-discipline? Ethical behavior as a rule requires effort. Responsibility and justice, for which Lipovetsky calls, tends to be difficult. To copy your homework is easier than doing it yourself. Resisting the temptation of a bribe is hard. If a student, official or politician has to be educated to be responsible—whether individually or socially—it will never happen without effort or pain. And if a person has to undergo some form of self-denial, that person must have a good, that is, meta-ethical, reason. In short, without meta-ethics, there is no ethics.

The cost we pay for the loss of meta-ethics is high not only from the philosophical point of view, but also from a purely pragmatic or practical stance. When we don't have anything on which to base a definition of good and evil, we must scrape together a consensual "package" of moral values which—in order to be universally acceptable—must be compromising, truncated, neutral, nor can it irritate or offend anyone. It has to be

20. Cf. ibid., 231.

politically correct. Only in this way can the neutralizations be sanctioned by any formal institution—in our part of the world that would be the one in Brussels, or at least by the Ministry of Education. Once that happens the prefabricated system of values is ready. It is safe, universal, copyable, teachable. It can be added to the school curriculum. But it has a hook. The implementation of "generic" values produces "generic" people. Let us consider a concrete educational problem. We would like children to acquire, as much as possible from the earliest age, empathy, since it is an important personal prerequisite for every moral action. But if empathy is cut off from a meta-ethical framework, it is defined according to the individual or social preferences of this or that culture. For example, if a child's prevailing culture is materialistic or hedonistic it can happen that empathy is nothing more than commiseration with other children who didn't get everything they wanted for Christmas. Or sympathy for the child whose parents made her go to music school, while "I didn't have to." Generic empathy will also have a problem distinguishing where to invest emotionally—to whom should we show our solidarity and offer our strength and resources? War refugees, victims of domestic violence, an endangered species of snails, or owners of weapons whose rights have been violated? Empathy defined on its own, i.e., unjustified by a meaning or purpose that transcends it, only with difficulty becomes a permanent and stable feature of a morally competent character. It can even become the exact opposite, as Bernard Williams noted: "If it is a mark of man to have a conceptualized and fully conscious awareness of himself as one among others, aware that others have feelings like himself, this is a precondition not only of benevolence but (as Nietzche pointed out) of cruelty as well."[21] If I know, because of empathy, how much it hurts you, I can really enjoy your pain.

The same applies to every ethical value and principle. If they are deprived of the meta-ethical anchor that would guarantee them an objective moral substance, they become subjective sentiments, moral judgments are no more than an expression of individual preferences and moral behavior is defined by individual choice. An individual without meta-ethics is of course capable of certain moral promises, but those promises must always be voluntary and painless. The individual can engage morally, but always reserves the right to disengage at any time.

To sum up—I submit that ethics is (specifically) three-dimensional, and therefore also that ethical education must develop the virtues of all

21. Williams, *Morality*, 64.

three dimensions. An ethical education, or a competent individual, is one who has 1) a good reason to behave well, 2) behaves well towards others, 3) behaves well alone (even when no one is looking). And one further note in conclusion. I have devoted considerable attention to meta-ethics in this chapter. The reason is obvious, but I repeat it again—without good meta-ethics there are no good ethics. Without a good "I am" there is no good "I am to be." At the same time I am aware that the reasons or meta-authority that would give sense to individual and social ethics have not yet been explicitly spelled out. I don't want to keep the reader in suspense, but I am leaving the answer to the final chapter, where I propose an alternative to our current non-meta-ethical education, with reference to the genius of J. A. Comenius's *methodus morum in specie*.[22]

22. This is what Comenius named the chapter on moral education in his *Great Didactic*.

Chapter 5

What Makes a Good Deed Good?

An apparently simple question. But our experience tells us that when any two people do the same thing, it's not the same thing. Theoreticians and practioners of ethics have long argued over it. Some are convinced the good should be good absolutely—always and everywhere and in every circumstance. Likewise with evil. Others think it is quite relative, conditional. Still others, that it is subjective, situational, and so on. I am convinced that it is even more complicated with human behavior, yet from a certain perspective it is more simple. It would be helpful to define moral behavior or moral acts. What does a good deed look like?

If an action is to be called moral or good, it must contain the following three components. It is necessary to keep in mind that all three form a complementary unity: if any of them is missing the moral quality of the act is nullified. *Essence, intention, situation.*[1]

The *essence*, or the nature of the act itself must be good. It is an objective factor of the act. Human actions have various natures; they are some way, in and of themselves, by their very nature—betrayal is evil, mercy is good, and so on. The quality of these actions can be changed in different ways, according to the circumstances and other factors—betrayal of a friend is different (worse) than betrayal of an enemy, mercy which is selfless is different (better) than that extended for gain. Before other factors can be attributed to an action it must fulfill the basic requirement—a good deed must be good by its nature. Betrayal, murder, and slander will always be evil.

1. The following paragraphs are free paraphrases from Thomas Aquinas. See his *Summa Theologica.*, I:II, ot. 18–22.

34

In some circumstances, they could perhaps be less evil, in others, more; but they will always be evil. The same goes with love, truthfulness, and bravery. I emphasize that the nature of an act is not the only moral factor, but it is the basic one, or it is foundational in the sense that without it the other factors would be groundless. The moral essence of an act flows from the existence of the moral law as an ontological entity, and expresses—I underline it again—the objective element in every moral deed.

The *intention*, or aim, purpose, or even motivation of the act must also be good. Morality does not happen only in the action, but also in the mind. The act is the result of a process that begins with the intention and is carried out by the will. Common moral intuition affirms that the motives of behavior—however subjective—are as important as the act itself. An evil motive ruins every act. Envy, greed, pride, and hatred morally disqualify every act, even when the act itself is good. For example, an act of solidarity with the poor is in itself considered good, but if the motivation for it is, say, the need to look good to others, the whole act loses its ethical quality; it is morally deficient. However, the logic of moral quality also goes in the opposite direction: a good motivation does not make a bad act good. Betrayal is still betrayal, even if it is done from a good motive. Once again the old saying applies: "The road to hell is paved with good intentions." A religious fanatic who fires a charge into a crowd may be genuinely convinced he is doing a good thing and therefore has a pure motive, but that sincere motive still doesn't make the act good. I highlight this in a later discussion: intention is a subjective element of moral behavior.

The *situation* or circumstance(s) must be good. Circumstances are a relative element of moral behavior. It's not always possible to control them, let alone anticipate them. They are often incidental to our actions, but nevertheless they play just as important a role as the previous two elements. A person can do the right thing, with good intentions, but if it is done in the wrong circumstances, the result is bad. Consequently the concordance of circumstances to the moral principles of human behavior gives them their moral quality—increasing and decreasing their value, and in diverse situations and circumstances creating diverse moral qualities for individual acts.[2] It is possible to distinguish at least four different qualifications of moral acts as a result of circumstances:

2. Cf. Schirrmacher, *Leadership*.

a) *The circumstances depreciate a good deed.* Helping a neighbor is undoubtedly a good thing. If, however, that neighbor is stealing from another neighbor and I unknowingly help him with the wheelbarrow, then that very circumstance of theft devalues my otherwise morally good act and motive.

b) *The circumstances make a good deed better.* It has already been said that some acts are good in and of themselves, but under certain circumstanaces they can become even better. Take the stories we tell ourselves and our children, to teach us: A wise master and teacher, who knew how to read the heart of a person, brought his disciples to the gate of the temple to watch the people giving their alms to the treasury. Many wealthy men came and threw in their entire purse. Then came a poor widow who gave her last penny. "Did you see that?" asked the teacher, "That woman gave the most." The disciples wanted to know how the teacher could say that, and he offered this thought: to give is a good thing, but the one who gave under the *circumstance* of her poverty gave more than the ones who gave out of their excess.[3] We hear similar points in many folk tales. The young girl was rewarded with a little pot which (magically) solved her social problems of deprivation and poverty after she shared her last slice of bread with an old woman. If she had a whole loaf of bread and gave the old woman five slices, the situation would have been better for the old woman—in terms of quantity, but the "situation" of it being the last slice gave the act a special quality.

c) *The circumstances make a bad deed worse.* Stealing is bad, but if the victim had little to start with or had just crashed his car, it's even worse. Again I offer a narrative illustration, which has for centuries cultivated a moral sense in its hearers: There once was a king. The court wiseman came to the king to tell him the story of two men in his kingdom. The first was a poor man who had nothing but one lamb who ate from his plate, drank from his cup, and was like a child to him. The second man had one hundred sheep. It happened that a friend came to visit the second man, who wanted to prepare a banquet for the friend but didn't want to use a sheep from his own herd. So he went and took the sheep from the first man, killed it, and prepared the banquet. When

---

3. Compare Luke's gospel, chapter 21, verses 1–4.

the king heard this he shouted, "Whoever did this must die!"[4] The point is clear—the circumstance of "the one sheep" made the consequences more serious, and therefore a deed which was already bad was made even worse.

d) *The circumstances soften the effect of a bad deed.* The well-thought-out theft of foreign property is morally more serious than stealing because of hunger. Similarly, a premeditated murder is more serious than killing someone inadvertently or in a deranged fit. Therefore the judicial system has the term "mitigating circumstances." There is another note to add to this last point. Among theoreticians of ethics there is an ongoing debate as to whether circumstances can not only mitigate the moral seriousness of a bad deed, but actually change its nature so that it becomes good. As examples they usually cite borderline moral dilemmas which force a choice between two evils, or an extreme (often violent) situation that makes lying, stealing or murder morally acceptable, or even desireable—for example, murdering a despot. Some think that "murdering a tyrant isn't murder," while others claim that circumstances don't change the moral nature of an act, they only qualify its value. Murder is murder even in an extreme situation, but in those extreme situations the act is less serious, or is morally understandable.

Moral action is thus a complex phenomenon. It is neither purely objective, nor purely subjective, nor purely relative. But if it is to be truly good, it must be good objectively, subjectively, and relatively at the same time. Good in its nature, good in its motivation, good in its circumstances. One can do the right thing but with a wrong intention. Another can have a pure motive, but ignore the nature of the act. And if we happen to do something that is good in its nature and its motivation, there are still circumstances which need to be taken into account at all times. Life often brings circumstances and situations which are simply not foreseeable. It turns out that to do a good deed, even just one—which includes all three components—is neither simple nor common at all. And that is so even in the case of a person making a conscious decision to have a good will: Today I will do a good deed. An example is the character of Ivan, from the well-known Russian Christmas tale Father Frost.[5] His preoccupation with himself so deformed

---

4. Freely taken from the Old Testament book of 2 Samuel, chapter 12.

5. For the version in English see https://www.youtube.com/watch?v=WA.sCujfg7VU.

his character that in the end he became inhuman, a monster and no longer a man. In order to become a man again he only had to do a "little thing," he had to do a good deed. He hurried to do just that, but try as he might, he couldn't complete one. Those who he wanted to help ran away in horror at the monster he had become. Eventually, he managed to help an old blind woman, which was a good deed by nature, and the circumstanaces were in Ivan's favor—the woman was weak and really needed help, and she was blind so she wasn't afraid of the monster. What was the problem? Ivan didn't have one of the components of moral behavior: his intentions were not good; he was doing the good deed with a self-centered motive. Only when Ivan forgot himself, and that was by accident, did he manage to do a good thing—he found the old woman's walking stick that she had lost in the forest, and picked it up to take to her because he knew she needed it. In that moment a miracle happened and the monster was changed back into a man. But Ivan didn't know that he had done his good deed. And the watchers or listeners to the story learn (among other things) that it is not enough just to do a good deed—they are presented with a complex example of how a human being becomes human(e). G. K. Chesterton and Vigen Guroian were right when they said that good fairy tales are basically textbooks of ethics.[6]

If it is so hard to accomplish one moral deed, what about moral behavior? Systematic, regular, over the long term. Individual acts that would develop into moral conduct and eventually become an integral part of human character. If some such person should appear, said Socrates somewhere, we would either love and worship that person, or kill him. Worship, because we would be in awe of the beauty and uniqueness of such a person. Kill him, because his perfection would contrast so sharply with our imperfection. In the light of perfect goodness our evil would be made clear, and we couldn't stand how that revealed goodness would irritate and annoy us.

But let us return to the topic. The above-mentioned components of moral behavior enable us to identify the three basic and most widespread ethical defects. I hesitate to call them theories, even though they appear in literature. In my judgment they are rather the faulty ethical positions, trends, or points of view, which—as a consequence of our moral imperfection—from time to time we all practice no matter what ethical theory we hold. The defect in the positions listed below is some disproportion between

6. See G. K. Chesterton, *Ortodoxie*; Guroian, *Tending of the Heart*.

essence, intention, and situation. When one of those factors is ignored, or given preference, an ethical defect appears.

1. *Legalism*—emphasizes only the nature of the act. The typical legalist doesn't acknowledge motives or circumstances, an act is either good or bad with nothing in between. From the lips of a legalist we might hear, "I didn't do anything illegal." And that is quite possibly true, even though the act was not moral.[7] We all are sometimes legalists, using rhetoric as a self-justifying strategy.

2. *Subjectivism* or emotivism—gives preference to only the second aspect. It doesn't complicate life with speculations about nature or situational factors. The deciding factor is motivation. From subjectivists we hear, "I meant it honestly." Well-meant intentions in and of themselves will never guarantee moral results.

3. *Situational ethics* (or *situationalism*)—adherents of this position claim that *a priori* moral principles don't exist, good and evil have no predetermined nature, it is set only in concrete situations. And because situations are so diverse, unpredictable, and relative, the categories of good and evil are themselves relative. Relativity is usually illustrated by dilemmatic situations in which a person is forced to choose between two evils and often doesn't know which is better. Critics of situational ethics point to the reality that such arguments lead to erroneous generalizations—it is not possible to extrapolate conclusions or principles for normal situations, from extreme ethical situations. In war people get killed, but war is an extreme situation and you can't deduce from it that it's okay for people to be killed anytime, that is, even under normal circumstances. If a child suffers from hunger as a result of poverty, it is possible that an otherwise upstanding father might be stealing his food. But does that mean that stealing is relative to the extent that it's okay to steal anytime? Even in normal situations?

The implications of these three components for ethical education are obvious. If good behavior is only good when the essence, intention, and situation of the behavior is good, it is necessary to pay attention pedagogically to all three levels.

---

7. An example is the situation when an individual discovers a loophole in the law and abuses the system in the spirit of "what isn't forbidden is allowed."

Essence. The child must first learn the moral basics, fundamental facts, laws, the alphabet of morality; to know that some things are naturally good and others not; to know where the boundaries are and how firm they are. The acquisition of moral knowledge is no different than acquiring any other kind of knowledge. A good teacher will initiate a child into the structure of moral reality with an eye towards the child's cognitive and developmental abilities—whether it's by direct or indirect method, play, instruction, demonstration, habits, examples, experience, or any other didactic strategy. Just as we teach children from their earliest years the names of things, shapes, meanings, colors, etc., we also teach them what is precious, valuable, true, good, and desireable. And not necessarily verbally or cognitively. Children (but not only them) for the most part learn moral principles and patterns primarily by imitation and later by identification. Thus it is not only what parents and teachers say, but primarily what they honor, praise, and live that become the subjects of imitation, appropriation, and identification on the part of the children. If the teachers themselves do not honor the moral values they verbalize or even demand, the learners will find them difficult to accept. They have a unique sensor that distinguishes even the tiniest dissonance between what those in authority say and what they do. If, however, the nature of the moral values and the attitudes of the educator are in harmony with the educator's conduct, the first necessary requirement for their acquisition has been fulfilled.

Intention. In addition to moral knowledge, ethical education must at the same time cultivate a motivation for ethical behavior. Not only to do the right thing, but to do it from the right motives; not only to know it well, but also to want it (Comenius even used the word "love"). Which requires a certain reflection—why do I do what I do? Also in this case the teacher must pay attention to the developmental potential of the children. Children in the heteronomic stage of development are not very concerned with their motives for their behavior, of course—they behave well because their authority (parent, teacher) requires it. It's natural that children themselves often don't want what is good, and only do it because the one in authority wants them to, or it will make them happy, or bring a reward. When moving into the autonomous stage, however, children begin taking responsibility for their own actions, and thus also for their motives. They themselves examine the nature of moral concepts, discovering that reality is a certain way, and is to be a certain (maybe different) way—and that they need to understand it for themselves. The role of the educator in this period is irreplaceable. In addition to the actual knowledge and experience the child simply does not yet have and needs to hear, the educator presents a moral example to the maturing individual. Both, the instruction and the example, are important. Individuals in this developmental stage might rebel against all authority, but they will notice the educator's moral contents and motives—they hear them, see them, and reflect on what they see and hear. Whether they accept them or not is always an open question, because many other factors also affect the educational process (peer groups, media, etc). But it seems that there are at least two fundamental prerequisites for the successful educational formation of an individual's moral motivation: a) a positive relationship between student and educator, and b) the moral integrity of the educator's own motives.

Situation. Given the wide variety of situations affecting the quality of moral education, it is clear that ethical education must develop the skill of applying moral principles to specific situations. Different situations require different applications of otherwise stable principles. The one principle of love requires an educator to sometimes reward and sometimes punish, because the one who does not punish (for example, arrogance or insolence) "hates their son"—as the old proverb says.[8] The art of applying moral principles in various situations is best learned by simply passing through, enduring, experiencing, and reflecting on individual situations. In the ideal case the teacher walks together with the student through real life situations and shows by example how to negotiate them. In the framework of school, the teacher has to mediate this didactically—narratively, through drama or other methods, and subsequently also to verbalize and think through moral situations and principles with the children. Of course, real situations are educationally always more effective.

8. Proverbs 13:24.

Chapter 6

Can Goodness Be Taught (and Learned)?

IN ONE OF HIS famous dialogues Plato has Meno raise the key question: Is it possible to teach virtue? And if yes, how? Through right knowledge? Or good habits? Is virtue natural to humankind? Or on the contrary, is it against human nature and it's necessary to somehow be retrained to it?[1]

Socrates's answer is deep and deserves careful consideration. Nevertheless at this moment I just want to draw the reader's attention to the intriging fact that in a few introductory interrogative sentences Plato almost prophetically names the four basic philosophies of education which people tested out over the following twenty-four centuries. 1) The most optimistic conception comes from the belief that people are by nature good, they become virtuous incidentally, naturally, and therefore no moral education is needed. The most famous proponent of this philosophy was Rousseau, mentioned previously, and many others followed him. 2) The second, also rather optimistic philosophy, assumed that a person becomes virtuous by right knowing. The one who finds true wisdom, or the knowledge of what is good, will also behave well. However, one must be properly led, taught, instructed, or enlightened to reach such knowledge. This is essentially Plato's approach, and with a specific emphasis on the autonomy of reason it is also Kant's. 3) The third educational approach states that virtue requires work and effort, it needs practice and habits. This is how Aristotle viewed it. In his judgment people are naturally neither bad nor good, but they should become good, and for that they need practice, action. A person becomes virtuous by behaving virtuously. 4) The final approach assumes that virtue

1. See Plato, *Euthydémos.*

is achieved against human nature. People are by nature immoral, selfish, like animals, and if they are to become good they must be compelled by force and fear, and thus tamed. We see this philosophy and anthropology in Hobbes, for example.

Which method or philosophy to choose? By which method should virtue be acquired? How to become good? In the dialogue mentioned above, Socrates admits that he doesn't know. That is for two reasons: first of all he doesn't know what virtue is—in contrast to Meno, who thought he knew, but in the following discussion discovered that in fact he didn't know. This is Socrates's standard didactic strategy—using dialogical questions to lead the student to the logical order of things. How could Meno want to know whether virtue was teachable when he didn't have a definition of what virtue is in the first place? This is lesson (and reason) number one, with which we must start—humble ignorance. The second reason for Socrates's ignorance also includes didactic intention. He says that even if we knew what virtue was, we don't have a teacher of virtue. Who is so virtuous that they could teach it to others? Socrates is pointing to the reality that even the most excellent men in history weren't able to teach virtue to their descendents. And in the end even Socrates himself admitted his own failure as a parent in this regard.

Where do we go from here? Did Socrates leave us without an answer? Yes and no. As a philosopher he wasn't a man of ready answers, but of curious questions that were primarily to reveal the supposed truths. Socrates sincerely didn't know, and therefore he questioned. And if one's ruminative questioning brings about the opportunity to uncover and admit their ignorance or error, they have already advanced significantly in their "study" of virtue. On the other hand, Socrates only indicates the path. In the conclusion of his dialogue he says that if there aren't any human teachers of virture, perhaps only a god could be the teacher. Such a statement can seem strange coming from the lips of someone who was sentenced to death for his godlessness which, according to the Athenian governors, was spoiling the youths. It is true that wherever Socrates walked he cast doubt on the Greek gods. But at the same time he spoke of the mysterious divine voice, which he judged to be above all gods and which gave the ability to identify right from wrong. The *daimonion* must be good because it advises Socrates to not listen to or obey the bad and corrupt gods. Even if all of Athens threatens him with death. Socrates will never obey corrupt gods.

His conscience will never allow it. When the *daimonion* speaks, it's necessary to obey.

From the time of Socrates, we as people have gone through a lot. Do we know today how to answer the question about teaching virtue? Teaching the good? The answer is complex, because the human situation is complex. Perhaps a small methodological excursion can help.

Chapter 7

An Excursion in Method
"Therapy" versus "Formation"

In the postwar twentieth century, schools in the Eastern block countries were undergoing a specific type of "ethical" education. It was straightforward totalitarian, ideological indoctrination. In Western countries, educational theoreticians had more freedom to experiment and test the mutations of some of Plato's previously-mentioned methods. With a little simplification, it's possible to summarize these moral-pedagogical trends into two main streams. On the one side is the philosophy of so-called *value clarification*, which is sometimes also called the *decision-making* method or the *critical thinking* method. Because all these pedagogies together have the common feature of a personalistic, non-directive or client-oriented approach to the individual, I will refer to them here as *therapeutic*. There are many proponents and advocates, but some of the most notable should be named: Carl Rogers, Jean Piaget, Lawrence Kohlberg, Sidney B. Simon, Louis Raths, and Merrill Harmin.

On the other (strongly opposed) side are the advocates of *character education* or *character development*, which is the approach that its supporters often identify as "traditional"[1] and its critics as "neoclassical."[2] Among the proponents are William Kilpatrick, Thomas Lickona, David Carr, Merle J. Schwartz, Peter Kreeft, Christina H. Sommers, and others. For a proper understanding of these approaches it's necessary to review the cultural-ideological context of their origin and dispute.

1. Kilpatrick, *Moral Illiteracy.*
2. Hunter, *Death.*

The Therapeutic Method and Its Critics

Education in the sense of therapeutic clarification of values (and all related concepts) was in many ways a reaction to the postwar crisis of values and culture in general. The coming generation openly distanced themselves from the "morals" of their parents. In addition to freedom of expression, emancipation of human rights and an emphasis on autonomy, the prevailing sentiment of the flower children was resistance towards the "stale" culture which priggishly preached, commissioned, and taught. The culture of their fathers—because of the horrors of war that were still fresh in their memories—had lost its moral legitimacy and become more of a source of shame than something to pass along pedagogically. From such a background it was not surprising, therefore, that in the 1960s there arose a method which had an emphasis on discussion, openness, engagement, no guidelines, and so on. The goal of the method was neither the formation nor transmission of any kind of specific "bag of virtues," in the words of Lawrence Kohlberg, or other moral material; that was indoctrination, which was considered one of the cardinal defects of all traditional educational approaches.[3] Teachers and educators of this new type were given the task of helping students to think independently and critically, based on the psychological assumption that if the individuals themselves identified their own values, the internalization of those values would be easier and more durable than if they were mediated by some adult. The students were thus guided to discover, classify, and develop their own values, that is, to construct their own moral universe.

Experimental findings by developmental psychologists such as Piaget and Kohlberg conveniently arrived just in time.[4] Although their theories of the moral and cognitive development of the individual were not originally intended to be educational, their application to pedagogy was soon found. Different variations of Kohlberg's famous micro-story dilemmas were used in lessons as a tool for clarifying moral categories and values, a tool from which was expected to both move the students to a higher stage of moral development, and teach them independent moral judgment and argumentation.

How does the method work in didactic practice? For illustration I present two mini-stories: Kohlberg's now famous "Heinz's Dilemma" and

3. See Hunter, *Death*, 219.
4. Cf. Piaget, *Moral Judgment*; Kohlberg, *Essays*.

"Sharon's Dilemma" from the just as well known teacher's handbook of Simon and his colleagues:[5]

> A fatally ill woman lived in Europe. She suffered from a special kind of cancer. There existed a medicine that was recently discovered by a pharmacist from the same town. To produce the medicine was very expensive, and the pharmacist charged ten times more than it cost him to make. Heinz, the husband of the sick woman, borrowed from everyone he could and still had only half of the cost of the medicine. He begged the pharmacist to lower the price or allow him to pay it in installments. But the pharmacist wouldn't budge. Desperate, Heinz broke into the pharmacy at night and stole the medicine.[6]

> Sharon and Jill were best friends. One day they went shopping together. Jill was trying on a sweater, when she suddenly put her jacket on over it and left the store. The guard arrived immediately afterwards, stopped Sharon and asked the name of her friend who had fled the store. At the same time, she threatened to call the police if Sharon wouldn't give the name.

The questions for discussion are obvious: Was Heinz's theft wrong or not? Should Sharon betray her friend or not? The discussion has to be well-controlled didactically in order to fulfill its task. Thefore the authors present the following instructions. 1) Recapitulate the basic facts of the story and ask a clear yes/no question. 2) Give the students enough time to think through the question and answer independently, ideally in writing, and with justification. 3) Next, the students say their answers aloud. If it happens that most of the group agrees, S. B. Simon recommends adding "balancing" information. For example, if most of the class votes for giving the name, the teacher can draw attention to the implications that would have on the girls' friendship, or bring a new variable into the story—for example, what if Jill was from a weak social background, and so on. 4) The teacher is to lead the discussion in a fundamentally non-directive manner. No interfering unless necessary, only steering it by means of questions—either stimulating (if the discussion lags), or regulatory (if the discussion gets off track) or clarifying (to break down concepts or motives, etc). Teachers must also avoid the temptation to express their own opinions (even though the students request it), because that usually ends the discussion. 5) The

5. I freely edited and shortened both stories.

6. Simon et al., *Values Clarification*.

conclusion of the discussion should contain a summary of the arguments (for and against), as well as a re-stating of the beginning and ending opinions. Did the students change their view? For what reason? And so on. Of course, the stories and strategies can also be subject to thematic changes and adapted to the age and circumstances of the group.

The method spread quickly and gained popularity. In addition to Simon's handbook, which became a bestseller, many other similar textbooks were published. By the 1980s, however, the first problems and criticisms had appeared. I will not here critique Kohlberg's theory as a diagnostic tool for identifying stages of moral development (others have already done that), but rather I will present a critique of the didactic application, since the subject of this book is moral education.

Critics admit this method brought about some contribution to the moral educational discussion. If it is used prudently, that is, sensitively choosing topics appropriate to the age and maturity of the children, circumstances, etc., this method can help make them sensitive to moral reality, sometimes even bringing them to a first "awakening"—from, for example, the typical adolescent egocentrism, or even narcissism. From the viewpoint of the content of the selected topics this method proved to be very attractive, especially in the critical teen years—what adolescent isn't interested in topics like sex, drugs, relationships, murders, or canibalism—eating the last survivor of a shipwreck on a deserted island. Non-directive and group strategies entertain, engage, or activate, and thus motivate and stimulate students, which is seen as the greatest didactic currency of this approach. But the criticism is massive.[7] I present here only a brief summary.

Process at the Expense of Content

The above-mentioned "family" of approaches to moral education suffers above all from the "subordination of content for the benefit of the process," says James Hunter. The presentation of certain moral content (*content-based instruction*) is secondary and completely overshadowed by questions about the "process whereby morality is acquired."[8] The ideological source of this approach is the anthropological assumption of the innate goodness of human nature, people are unproblematically good—ontologically and

7. See, for example, Gilligan, *Different Voice*; Dykstra, *Vision*; Atherton, *Kohlberg*; Hunter, *Death*.

8. Hunter, *Death*, 177–78.

morally—just as Rousseau said. In the twentieth century we first saw this dominance of process over content in Carl Rogers's personalistic concept of client-centered therapy. Rogers says that people should accept themselves as "streams of becoming" in a life-long process of self-actualization. Fully actualized individuals would then see themselves as a "fluid process, not a fixed and static entity . . . a continually changing constellation of potentialities, not a fixed quantity of traits."[9] Later Rogers explicitly states that the process of self-realization applies to education as much as to therapy. "The teacher," says Rogers, "becomes a facilitator in the process of the students' self-definition . . . , a resource-finder . . . He would want the quality of his relationship to the group to be such that his feelings could be freely available to them, without being imposed on them or becoming a restrictive influence on them."[10]

This emphasis was enthusiastically corroborated by many educators. William Glasser, for example, in his book *School Without Failure* bluntly condemns education aimed at specific moral content as preaching. "We teach mindless conformity to *school* rules and call the conforming child 'responsible.'"[11] Simon et al. speak in a similarly unequivocal way when they say that contents of a traditional curriculum are "out-dated, moralistic," and strive after the "inculcation of adult values into the youth," and as such are "indoctrination." They, in contrast, seek a higher goal, "the facilitation of the process of moral judgment."[12] The same appeal comes from the constructivist camp. A school that would present any kind of "objective morality" is compared to an "army camp," and the teachers to "drill sergeants." Proper education should consist of drawing out values only "as the need arises," say Rheta DeVries and Betty Zan. They continue, "We are talking here about a process and not a product. In this process, children wrestle with questions, what to believe to be good and bad, right and wrong. They form their own opinions, and listen to the opinions of others. They construct their own morality out of daily life experiences."[13] The last thing a teacher should do is to "dictate moral norms to the children."[14] Instead, a

---

9. Rogers, *On Becoming*, 122.

10. Ibid., 289.

11. Glasser, *School*, 186.

12. Simon et al., *Values Clarification*, 15–16.

13. DeVries and Zan, *Moral Classrooms*, 28.

14. Ibid., 132.

teacher should "cooperate with the children by trying to understand their reasoning and facilitating the constructive process."[15]

However understandable is the resistance to traditional moral content, and however welcome the appeal for a helpful pedagogical climate, the unilateral emphasis on the procedural side of moral formation has had the effect over time of emptying the contents of moral education as such. The logic of the problem is simple. If the teacher only therapeutically "recognizes, accepts and validates"[16] the students' moral feelings and perceptions without resorting to criticism (because it would improperly interfere with the students' process of self-actualization), it's inevitable that sooner or later the teacher will agree with a completely immoral construction on the side of the student. Which has also been confirmed in pedagogical practice. Thomas Lickona recalls from his clinical research the experience of a 9th grade teacher who, within the framework of ethical education, used the technique of "voting on values." The teacher began the discussion with the question "Who of you has ever stolen something from a store?" Most of the students raised their hands. "Don't you think that stealing is bad?" Lickona comments that the teacher forgot for a moment that such a question violates the rule of value neutrality. "We have a right to material things," answered one of the students, and the others nodded in agreement.[17] The teacher remained clueless.

In addition to similar narrative testimonies there are many empirical studies which unsurprisingly support that the *suppression* of the *content* of education leads logically to its emptying of content, and ultimately to its malfunctioning.[18] If the individual is not exposed to moral content there is nothing to develop; moral development simply does not appear.

Devaluation of the Authority of the Educator

The imperative of therapeutic non-instruction is not only a matter of the teachers' didactic manner or conduct in the classroom, it basically concerns their social role. Proponents of the methods described above encourage educators to programmatically abdicate their traditional role as ones who instruct, interpret, and present moral content. We have seen a shift

15. Ibid., 78.
16. Hunter, *Death*, 181.
17. Lickona, *Educating*, 11.
18. Kilpatrick, *Moral Illiteracy*.

in the understanding of their role—the teacher should act as a facilitator or consultant, sometimes an assistant. They still have the responsibility of organizing classroom activities and academic discipline, but the way of accomplishing it is different under the therapeutic conception. In 1963 Jean Piaget said that the "imposition of the authority" of an adult is, in an educational context, "absurd" and "immoral." In his judgment, an adult should only be an "elder collaborator and, if he has it in him, a simple comrade" to children.[19]

The same philosophy applied in Kohlberg's experimental community (*Just Community*)—"students and teachers participate equally in the creation and enforcement of rules."[20] Parents are also encouraged to take the same approach: "To achieve [the] parental goal of raising responsible children who grow into responsible men and women, parent-child relationships need to be based on democratic principles . . . of mutual respect and equality."[21] To this James Hunter observes that the term "democracy" is used here, but it's losing its specific historical meaning. The original—Greek—usage of the term expressed a way of organizing the political life of a society where the roles and relational responsibilities between the people (*démos*), and those who lead them, were defined in a concrete way. But educational therapeuticians use the term democracy without that context, and here it describes the process of social organization without any further identification. Thus it becomes a code or charm legitimizing the right of individuals to participate and make decisions in any context.[22] The consequences are predictable. The established structure of pedagogical authority loses its social significance.

Blurring of Concepts and Standards

The growing reluctance to convey any kind of moral content, however objective, accompanied by the phenomenon of weakened teacher authority to safeguard the content, had the effect of eroding moral terminology and, ultimately, moral standards as such. As in theory, so in practice, the normative distinctions for seeing and clarifying good from evil were lost. The concepts of good and evil, right and wrong did not completely disappear,

19. Taken from Power, "Democratic Schools," 319.
20. Power, et al., *Lawrence Kohlberg*, 62.
21. Dinkmeyer, et al., *Handbook*, 5.
22. Cf. Hunter, *Death*, 182.

but were redefined, which caused a fatal confusion of terminology and was a source of misunderstanding.

When, for example, Kohlberg talks about morality or immorality, they are always relative terms, defined according to the level of moral judgment the individuals are capable of using in this or that period of their development. So as people evolve they become more "moral;" it's not the same as becoming good. For example, if selfishness or other character flaws appear in the judgment or behavior of individuals, it's the result of developmental or cognitive immaturity, or general inadequacy in their cognitive functionality.[23] Once again we see the same assumptions that we saw earlier in Rousseau—evil, depravity, and wrong are not inherent, natural, or lasting characteristics of human nature. The concept of good and evil has lost its ontological status, and with that also, its objective meaning and gradually also, its meaningful referential framework in language, which Alasdair MacIntyre very aptly pointed out.[24] Today the terminological "fog" is obvious not only to the experts; note the line from the popular 2012 film, *Cloud Atlas*: "Do you want to know truth or true truth?"

In the therapeutic context, the concepts of *good* and *evil* have slowly become outdated and incorrect, precisely because they have lost their ability to relate to anything that would be considered as moral reality. Adam Philips notes that the therapeutic approaches have literally developed a "phobia" to the word *evil*.[25] I have personally observed a similar fate for the word *guilt*. The fact that there is a pathological form of this "emotion" has led to its stigmatization and the subsequent neglect of its healthy form. At the same time, the psychological strength of guilt is, in terms of healthy moral development, irreplaceable. It has the "power" to save people from

23. Cf. Ibid., 183.

24. MacIntyre's book, with the title *Ztráta ctnosti* [After virtue], first published in 1981, presents a "disturbing hypothesis" about the current state of moral discourse. Entire and coherent conceptual systems have disappeared, according to MacIntyre, and in their place we have only fragmented sayings and partial beliefs. The cause is not the decline of morality in a superficial sense, but the deeper decay of meaningful moral language into which these fragments could be put and rationally developed. MacIntyre believes this decline is connected to the expansion of modern individualistic morality. He shows that moral emotivism has degraded every moral statement into a mere expression of individual preference. All statements like "it should be" or "it's right" can be decoded and reveal someone's will behind them. In continenal philosophy, the parallel to emotivism is primarily Friedrich Nietzsche's conception of morality. MacIntyre opposes both concepts and argues that they are only a reflection of the state of moral language after its decline in the modernity, especially in the Enlightenment.

25. Philips, *Flirtation*, 59.

their tendency towards wrong behavior, and also to motivate them towards correction when a wrong has been committed. But this potential is dependent on a shared concensus on the concepts of good and evil. By eliminating it, the concept of guilt has become powerless and forbidden. The guilty one needs therapy, not punishment.

Hunter adds that neologisms such as the word *prosocial* are an unconcealed attempt to avoid the encumbrance of the old moral categories.[26] In principle, the meaning remains the same—socially positive or negative behavior matches with the statement "what you did is good/bad," but the hard emotional tip of the concepts are broken off, and in addition the teachers are enabled to distance themselves from terminology which sounds judging or condemning. This is well illustrated by the fact that the frequent use of the term *prosocial* didn't used to be contrasted in literature with the word *evil*, or with *antisocial*. Rather it was contraseted with the somewhat amorphous word *negative*, in discussions about the deficiencies of prosocialism. But never to talk about *evil*.[27]

If the moral concepts still appear in linguistic usage, then it is only as categories of meaning which individuals construct on the basis of their experience. Teachers then have the task of encouraging students in that construction of moral reality, for example, by programmatically creating the opportunity to vote on rules for classroom behavior, or the values that will become the code of the group. But what happens when the students—in their predictable invention and creativity—vote, say, that someone who doesn't cheat is a "chicken," or maybe that they don't wish to do certain school activities that require effort, such as grammar lessons or PE, on the grounds that they don't belong to their value system?

The obfuscation of moral language is also evidenced by pedagogical practice based on the therapeutic approach. Critics point out that the fundamental misgivings and danger of the method of moral dilemmas consists in its implicit relativization of moral principles. If students are programmatically exposed to unsolvable moral situations, they can get the impression that all morality is "unsolvable," i.e., problematic, controversial, and ultimately relative. Students who are confronted with one extreme situation after another in which it isn't clear whether they should steal, lie, kill, or eat each other, in the end become convinced that concepts such as good and evil are completely vague. Which is a very sophisticated form of

26. Hunter, *Death*, 183.
27. Cf. ibid.

indoctrination, because it is carried out on a latent level.[28] But is the starting point of this premise of this approach correct? Is it possible to apply conclusions derived from extreme situations to non-extreme situations? From abnormal to normal? From exceptional to common? Let us consider the example of Heinz's dilemma. In a life and death situation stealing seems acceptable, even moral—what would it be for a person who puts morals (not stealing) above human life? Does it follow from these extremes that stealing is permissible—even under ordinary (or all) circumstances? The answer is obvious (at least I hope so). And I believe that neither Kohlberg nor any other supporters of the critical method would agree with a conclusion of unrestrained robbery. Nevertheless, the method of moral dilemmas really leads to such a conclusion, even if the teacher is not aware of it.

Kilpatrick wonders how a dilemma about theft could help young teenagers overcome the temptation to steal money from their parent's wallet. He says that most of the moral situations faced by both children and adults are not dilemmas, most moral choices are unambiguous. We simply have to do what we know we should do, and not do what we know we shouldn't. The time spent in school would be much better used by considering (and practicing) virtues such as friendship, loyalty, and honesty, rather than focusing on unsolvable situations where truthfulness seems wrong, friendship is separated from honesty, and cannibalism is legitimized.[29] Kilpatrick further notes that the method of dilemmas, especially when applied to children at an early stage of moral and cognitive development, is "woefully inadequate," because it comes out of the assumption that children already have the "ABCs of morality," and are therefore able to cope with questions requiring a higher level of moral judgment. In other words, Kilpatrick is arguing that before children are exposed to moral complexity (remember Sharon: "Is it right to be loyal to a friend, or truthful to the authorities?"), they should be taught the basics of morality ("Is it right to steal this sweater?"). If that doesn't happen the youth are put into moral confusion, because they are instilled with the preconceptions that a) suppress the basic moral intuition that some things are really and unproblematically good and some bad; b) lead to a contradiction between moral theory and moral practice. However possible it is to instill and hold the *theory* of the relativity of moral norms, it cannot be meaningfully applied in *practice*. We start teaching children from the time they're in the sandbox that there are some things they cannot do to others, and we say the same thing to criminals in court.

28. Cf. Thiessen, *Teaching*.
29. Kilpatrick, *Moral Illiteracy*, 85–86.

Individualism, Subjectivism, Relativism

In light of what has been said it is unsurprising that therapeutic pedagogy has earned accusations of moral subjectivism, accompanied by individualism, and eventually leading to moral relativism. Conservative theoreticians and practioners of education have been thoroughly heard from in this respect. See, for example, Kilpatrick's bestseller, *Why Johnny Can't Tell Right From Wrong*, first published in 1992. In the title the author makes a deliberate reference to the earlier book by Rudolf Flesch, *Why Johnny Can't Read*. In it, Flesch clarifies the reason for the failure of certain didactic experiments carried out in America in the postwar years. Briefly, the traditional phonetic method of language teaching was replaced by the "look-say" method, in which the focus of reading acquisition was transferred from teachers to students. The authors of the project promised greater engagement of students, which would lead to more effective acquisition of reading skills. The reality was just the opposite and the project was a total failure, but before it ended (for a certain time it had the approval of the federal authorities), it produced a whole generation of nearly illiterate "readers." Kilpatrick says that something similar happened in the area of moral education. In his judgment, the dramatic decline in moral literacy, which can not only be documented statistically but also seen with the naked eye, is the consequence of implementing a bad method. A whole generation of children have been fooled by its moral relativism, and are now unable to recognize the good from the bad.

Proponents of therapeutic pedagogy defend themselves against the accusation of relativism. They say that their method "definitely promotes the values of thinking, feeling, choosing, communicating, and acting," and elsewhere, "rationality, justice, creativity, autonomy, and equality."[30] Alfie Kohn denounces the "rampant individualism and self-assurance" that threaten society as a whole, and argues for "community cooperation" as a key goal of moral education.[31] Abraham Maslow similarly expresses that "valuelessness" is the "greatest disease of our time."[32] The term *democracy* also often appears as a non-negotiable value which should be promoted by moral or civic education. (There is even a subject called Education to Democracy, or Democratic Thinking—as opposed to totalitarian thinking).

---

30. Kirschenbaum, *Advanced*, 12–13.

31. Kohn, "The Truth," 272–83.

32. Maslow, *Psychology*, 133.

And the same goes with *respect, tolerance, empathy,* and the so-called *Golden Rule.*[33] So, no relativism.

It is good, however, to ask all these sets of values the question: where are they coming from? On what ontological basis do they stand? How are they anchored or validated? One way to avoid meta-ethical problems is simply to assert that they are values of the type of universal maxims or ideals that are self-validating or self-evident, and no further justification is needed. But such an evasive maneuver doesn't work in education. From the earliest age children are wired in such a way as to need to know the reasons for their actions, or the actions required of them. The instruction "you should" do this or that, or behave in this way or that, calls forth a child-like natural and unaffected desire to know *why.* It's true that there are "why" questions and developmental stages that really don't need an answer, such as "Why shouldn't I touch the burner?" But others literally cry out for an answer: "Why should I be brave?" "Why must I control myself?"

Most educators know this very well, and therefore, if possible, they look for good answers or fundamentals which would give meaningful justification for moral values and rights. Including therapeutic educators. But on what basis? Moral ideals are rooted "neither in the conventions of social life or public discourse, nor in an external or transcendent standard inherited from any particular moral tradition," explains Hunter, and he continues, "rather, these ideals are rooted in the rights (the desires, feelings, needs and potentialities) of the autonomous individual. The self, in brief, is both the source of all moral sensibility and the final object of moral accountability."[34] Rogers can in many ways be considered the father of this concept:

> The individual increasingly comes to feel that the locus of evaluation lies within himself. Less and less does he look to others for approval or disapproval; for the standards to live by; for decisions and choices. He recognizes that it rests within himself to choose; that the only question that matters is "Am I living in a way that is deeply satisfying to me, and which truly expresses me?"[35]

Elsewhere he adds:

> Everyone possesses the capacity to expand, extend, become autonomous, develop, mature. [Moral capacity] exists in every

33. Hunter, *Death,* 188.
34. Ibid.
35. Rogers, *Becoming,* 119.

individual and awaits only the proper conditions to be released and expressed ... Whether one calls it a growth tendency, a drive toward self-actualization, or a forward-moving directional tendency, it is the main-spring of life.[36]

In psychotherapeutic circles Maslow speaks similarly about people. Everyone has an "inner core" which "as much as we know of it so far, is definitely not 'evil,' but is either what we adults in our culture call 'good' or else it is neutral," he explains.[37] "Self-realization" and "self-fulfillment" are, in his judgment, "instinctive." Let Maslow speak more extensively about human nature:

> Man demonstrates in his own nature a pressure towards fuller and fuller Being, more and more perfect actualization of his humanness in exactly the same naturalistic, scientific sense that an acorn may be said to be "pressing toward" being an oak tree, or a tiger can be observed to "push toward" being tigerish, or a horse toward being equine. Man is ultimately not molded or shaped into humanness or taught to be human. The role of the environment is ultimately to permit him or help him to actualize his own potentialities.[38]

Rousseau would have rejoiced: *no molding, no teaching, permission, letting the potential itself be actualized* ... What potential? "Creativeness, spontaneity, selfhood, authenticity, caring for others, being able to love, yearning for truth are embryonic potentialities belonging to his species-membership just as much as are his arm and legs and brain and eyes."[39]

The therapeutical educational concepts are, in their theory, true echoes of this anthropology. Again and again we read that, "learning is a process whereby meaning, ethical or otherwise, must be actively invented and reinvented, from the inside out."[40] Or other authors: "The individual who is antonomously moral follows moral rules of the self. Such rules are self-constructed, self-regulating principles."[41] Hence the didactic emphasis on autonomous decision-making and choice, which are so characteristic of this kind of education. True values "represent the free and

36. Ibid., 9.

37. Maslow, "Psychological Data," 130.

38. Ibid.

39. Ibid.

40. Kohn, "How Not to Teach," 429–33.

41. DeVries and Zan, *Moral Classrooms*, 46.

thoughtful choice of intelligent humans interacting with complex and changing environments."[42] But the values must be chosen freely, else they're not "right." Or, at least, "chosen from among alternatives," but mainly, "after independent consideration." The imperative for free choice has become so inviolable that educators have been encouraged to "help the children look for value, *as long as* [emphasis mine] the children make the decisions. It is also possible that the children decide to not develop values. The teachers' responsibility is to support even such a decision."[43] Kohn adds pregnantly: "children must be invited to reflect on complex issues, to recast them in the light of their own experience and questions, to figure out for themselves— and with one another—what kind of person one ought to be."[44] In other words, a value can become one's own only through choice.

Pedocentrism of this type necessarily leads to moral subjectivism and relativism. It is well illustrated by the handbook of one of the therapeutic education programs with the title *Growing Up Caring*. Let's consider two examples. In the chapter on cheating in school a student discovers a picture of a girl during an exam looking over the shoulder of her classmate, with the accompanying text: "Cheating, in any form, is bad for your self-esteem." In another chapter in the book is a photograph of a young girl who is stealing from a store, while the next picture shows two other people watching her and recording it on camera. The accompanying text says: "One way to test the impact a decision will have on your feeling of self-worth is to imagine a picture being taken of you implementing your decision."[45] The ethical argument of these instructions is clear—the children are not led to believe that cheating or stealing are objectively wrong because they violate a universal law. Cheating is wrong because it calls forth an unpleasant feeling, or threatens the self-confidence of an individual. Such an argument is almost amusing to someone who grew up under a totalitarian regime in the seventies and eighties. In a culture deformed by Communist ideology people felt downright happy if they could manage to steal from state-owned property, or at least get around some law. After all, the best people—from a moral perspective—were usually "illegal" or in prison or exile. Things are different now in both the East and the West. The "feeling" argument no longer works today—the number of individuals whose self-esteem would

42. Raths, et al., *Values*, 41.
43. Ibid., 48.
44. Kohn, "How Not to Teach," 435.
45. Hunter, *Death*, 122–23.

be lowered by being exposed as a person who committed an unethical act is rapidly declining everywhere.

Subjectivism, which is behind the therapeutic concepts of pedagogy, has a direct connection with the "cultures" of ethical utilitarianism and emotivism (sometimes called expressionism). In utilitarianism, moral discourse determines the logic of expediency and usefulness, in emotionalism the logic of psychological well-being. In both cases it is the individual I who arbitrates moral prudence. In this frame of reference, the most important moral act is that of choice. Making a decision. Not a decision *for something*, just making a decision, period. And decide it yourself. Jean Paul Sartre in pedagogical robes.

The results? Therapeutic pedagogies have achieved their goals, and in doing so have become part of the problem they wanted to solve. The therapeutically raised generation is truly autonomous, at least to the extent that they have ruled out any commitment that would go beyond the borders of subjective choice and personal well-being. It is the logical result of programmatic questioning of objective moral reality. If I am being convinced that the final arbiter of moral values is me, or my feelings, eventually I will believe it. If I am methodically urged to self-identify my existence through free choice, I will eventually do it. Who would have expected that, entirely freely, I would choose evil? But it could have been expected—at least since Zimbard and Milgram.[46] But before them Dostoyevsky already said it, and before him Aquinas, Augustine, Paul of Tarsus and many others.

The "Abolition of Man"

When talking about subjectivism, it is impossible to ignore the criticism that C. S. Lewis presented in a completely unique way in his book *The Abolition of Man*, subtitled *Reflections on Education with Special Reference to the Teaching of English in the Upper Forms of Schools*. Lewis's treatise crosses lines not only in its form—concise, intense, brief, and all with typical Lewis readability—but most of all in that Lewis almost prophetically predicted the moral problems that came later. Most observers and critics—including

---

46. Much has been written about the so-called prison experiment of Philip Zimbard (it was even filmed), and likewise about Stanley Milgram's study of human conformity. For details on Zimbard, see, for example, the home page of the Stanford experiment: http://www.prisonexp.org/. On Milgram, see his *Obedience to Authority*. The goal of these experiments was to study why, how, and under what circumstances people choose evil.

those I refer to here—normally analyze the results of some phenomenon; but Lewis, with unprecedented foresight, presented a description of what was yet to come. Therefore, he deserves special attention.

The text of the book is based on three lectures Lewis gave in 1943.[47] Lewis is reacting to a textbook on the English language which—so it wouldn't offend anyone—was hidden under the designation "green book" by the pseudonymous authors "Gaius and Titus." It was a book written in 1939 called *The Control of Language: A Critical Approach to Reading and Writing*, by Alex King and Martin Ketley. Lewis analyzes the way in which the authors of the textbook subvert the students' values—not only the moral ones. When a value statement is made, such as "that waterfall is beautiful," the authors teach that it is only the subjective statement of a specific feeling on the part of the observer, not a statement about objective reality. We think we're saying something important about something real, but we are actually only saying something about our own feelings, claim the authors. Lewis argues that such subjectivism in value judgments is flawed, because some subjects and some acts are actually real; that is, they are objective and deserve an evaluation, whether positive or negative. A waterfall is objectively beautiful, a villain is objectively evil. Understandably, an ethics which doesn't believe in the reality of objective moral values will avoid the concepts of good and evil. But if we replace "good" with predicates like "necessary," "progressive," or "impressive," it is just a trick of language, a linguistic ruse, says Lewis, explaining with the questions: "necessary for what? progressing towards what? effecting what? in the last resort they [Gaius and Titus] would have to admit that some state of affairs was in their opinion good for its own sake." In other words—it is good to call things by their right names and cultivate an "ethics without predicates."

According to Lewis, this ethics has been well taught by good teachers from time immemorial. Lewis reminds us of the thinkers of antiquity such as Plato, Aristotle, and Augustine, who, in one way or another cultivated "ordinate affections," that is, teaching people to love that which ought to be loved and to hate that which ought to be hated. To love good and hate evil. Although moral feelings and values are real, they don't develop automatically in people, says Lewis. Hence the need for education. Those who don't have these moral capacities are lacking the very thing that would make them specifically human. They would be, in Lewis's words, "men without chests" or "without hearts." The Gaius and Titus book produces such people

---

47. I will not burden the text with heavy referencing. All the quotations are taken from Lewis, *Abolition of Man*.

by undermining the fact that people are capable of contact with objective reality (moral, aesthetic, or other), thus taking away from them that which is humanly the most valuable. Do you think there is something real outside of you? Truth, goodness, beauty, the *noumena*? Wrong. There's only you. The subject. Your impression. Phenomena. Illusion.

What will happen with the human world when we explain away and thus domesticate moral reality? In the last part of his book Lewis gives an unbelieveably accurate sketch of the contours of the modern dystopia which should soon emerge, if this demoralizing trend continues. The power of human beings to do exactly what they wish will grow with the so-called "conquest of nature," that is, the development of the natural sciences. However, every new power acquired by "Man" is, at the same time, "power over man," says Lewis. Therefore, it is good to ask whose power grows with every further sublimation of nature. Lewis predicts that if the dream of some scientists becomes a reality and we humans "take control of nature," it will mean the supremacy of hundreds of people over billions of others. The final stage of conquest will be conquest of one's self, that is, human nature. Human nature will be the final bastion of the natural world that will be conquered. The victorious ruling minority will become a caste of Conditioners, that is people who will have control tools (he mentions eugenetics, genetics, and psychology), and who will knead, form, and cut out the nature of the succeeding generations however they want. "The process which, if not checked, will abolish Man goes on apace among Communists and Democrats no less than among Fascists," warns Lewis, I remind the reader, in 1943. "The methods may (at first) differ in brutality. . . . The belief that we can invent ideologies at pleasure, and the consequent treatment of mankind as mere specimens, preparations, begins to affect our very language." Man's conquest of Nature turns out to be Nature's conquest of Man. Man's power over everything destroys him.

Lewis called the process of conquering, when people sacrifice one thing after another, and finally even themselves, in order to gain power over nature and human nature, a "magician's bargain." Faust's metaphor illustrates the fact that modern "science" has the same goal as ancient magic, which is the submission of reality to the wishes of humankind. To command the wind and the rain. To gain *that hideous strength*,[48] which is in fact to become a god. To achieve their goal, magic and science are prepared to do things that have long been considered "disgusting and impious."

---

48. I am referring to one of Lewis's books of fiction, called *That Hideous Strength*, which narratively portrays this problem.

This also applies to moral values and principles. If they are conquered, people will have the power to freely modify, design, and even produce them. Moral values and ethics are not things that determine a person, but things that people themselves determine however they see fit. Which means the end of them. And this is the "tragi-comedy of our situation," Lewis concludes: we call loudly for precisely those qualities that we ourselves have subverted. "In a sort of ghastly simplicity we remove the organ and demand the function. We make men without chests and expect of them virtue and enterprise. We laugh at honour and are shocked to find traitors in our midst. We castrate and bid the geldings be fruitful."

Value Pseudo-neutrality and Indoctrination

Critics of therapeutic pedagogy point to the fact that, in spite of their claim that the therapeutic approach is completely value-neutral, the reality is the opposite. Kilpatrick presents an example of a favorite didactic strategy, "VV," which is Value Voting.[49] The exercise begins with innocent questions like "How many of you like to go for walks in the countryside?" or How many of you love picnics?" or "How many of you love yogurt?" But soon there appear questions like "How many of you approve of premarital sex?" or "Which of you are for legalizing abortion?" or "How many of you are in favor of having homosexual couples married by priests, ministers, and rabbis?" Kilpatrick points out that the authors of the method have made no effort to separate the heavy value questions from the light ones. They are intertwined as though there were no significant differences between them. The exercise is designed to give young people the impression that "all values are questions of personal taste—as in the case of yogurt," says Kilpatrick. This kind of design is not only not neutral, it is "indoctrinating" because it deliberately and somewhat deceitfully instills the doctrine of *value relativity*. Whether or not it is the teachers' intention, if this method is used in pedagogical practice it does indoctrinate (although they usually are not even aware of it).

Proponents of the therapeutic method understandably don't like to be associated with such a—for them almost vulgar—word and vehemently defend themselves.[50] Indeed, resistance to indoctrination was one of the

49. Kilpatrick, *Moral Illiteracy*, 81–82.

50. See, for example, Kohlberg, "Just Community," 32, 34–35, or Downey and Kelley, *Moral Education*.

central motives of the alternative approach. But the problem is that they defined the term indoctrination very vaguely. It didn't occur to them that they also held a set of specific values and doctrines which they perforce communicated to children, by whatever indirect method. Once the term is defined it becomes clear that their approach fulfills every criteria of indoctrination. The definition of Downey and Kelley, to which Kohlberg referred in one of his apologies, is an illustration of the problem. The triad of indoctrinating criteria—questionable content, questionable method, questionable goals—is so general that even its proponents fall into it. They communicate notoriously questionable content or doctrine—values are relative. They use questionable methods—the therapeutists preferred non-directive methods of teaching; non-directiveness, however, doesn't guarantee anything. Teachers may (and often do) indoctrinate in a non-directive way.[51]

That is, in effect, an effective trick. Intentional, asks Kilpatrick?[52] I won't be as mistrustful as my colleague here. I use the adjective effective as opposed to intentional, because I am not presuming that there is any premeditated or manipulative intent. On the basis of my own pedagogical experience and personal interaction with fellow teachers, I have come to the conclusion that few teachers actually seek to relativize moral values on the part of their students. Rather, I think that users of the therapeutic method simply haven't anticipated the implications of their theory. There is nothing more practical than good theory. If, however, the theory is dubious, the practical consequences will be dubious too, even though the way is lined with good intentions.

Not only the teacher, but also the student is outwitted here. They were promised a tool to "stimulate" moral thinking which would lead to greater moral competence, but in reality they were subjected to the process of methodological relativization of values. It is woven into the therapeutic textbooks, not in a neutral way, but skillfully (and probably unintentionally) hidden. Despite the rhetoric of value neutrality that it proclaims in theory, practice shows that the therapeutic educator is anything but neutral.

---

51. Kohlberg, "Just Community," 34–35. I will deal with the question of indoctrination later. For now it is enough to suggest that there are a lot of more sophisticated definitions with finer criteria such as evidential, relational, rational, or emotional use of methods which in some way abuse or hide evidence, rationality, relationships between teacher and student, etc. For further details see Thiessen, *Teaching*.

52. Kilpatrick, *Moral Illiteracy*, 82.

Problematic Autonomy

The imperative for autonomy that therapeutic pedagogy has emphasized as a goal is understandable, and to a large extent even legitimate, especially when we consider the opposite—a dependent, unsure, insecure, compliant, etc. individual. We have seen in the previous chapters that the term *autonomy* has been used so frequently it has become an accepted part of pedagogical terminology, without anyone having been too careful about a positive definition. To define the term negatively is relatively simple—what we are not and don't want to be—but to offer positive content is more difficult. The synonyms we encounter in the pedagogical manuals, like self-determination, independence, and freedom are alright, but they are only synonyms, not definitions. What does it actually mean to be independent? Free? Self-determined?

The word autonomy makes sense in its original historical context, when the Greeks defined it as the free status of a city which was not under the control of a conqueror. But what kind of meaning does it have when it's applied to a person? Halsted points out that with people it is a metaphorically used term, and as with all metaphors, it is not easily defined.[53] The versatility of the term is evident from the number of attributes attached to it. We speak on the one hand of moral autonomy, and on the other hand of institutional autonomy, or rational, and so on. Keith Ward lists sixteen different kinds of autonomy.[54] A careful reading of pedagogical texts reveals that educators routinely go from one metaphor to another, so I will attempt to name and summarize the ideal of a morally autonomous individual, as it appears in pedagogical literature.

1. *Freedom.* An autonomous individual is free, and free (in this context) usually means "the absence of constraints or restraints relevant to what we do or might want to do."[55]

2. *Independence.* Autonomous individuals have their own opinion and behave according to it. "They accept or make rules for themselves. They are capable of forming their own independent judgements. Their thoughts and actions are not governed by other people, by tradition, by authority, or by psychological problems."[56]

53. Halstead, *Muslim*, 34.
54. Ward, "Autonomy?"
55. Deardon, "Autonomy," 450.
56. Thiessen, *Teaching*, 118.

3. *Self-control.* Autonomous individuals are not "swamped" by their own passions or needs. They are able to arrange and adjust their desires, ideals, and goals corresponding to "a hierarchical structure of some life plan."[57]

4. *Rational reflection.* Autonomous individuals contemplate and consciously think over what they do and who they believe. They subjugate their actions and convictions to reflection and criticisms. They are endowed with the sufficient and necessary knowledge to make intelligent decisions.

5. *Competence.* Autonomous individuals are able to implement the plans and projects they have made. They posses volition, determination, and every other "executive virtue" necessary for autonomous behavior.[58]

6. *Final note:* There is a consensus among educators that a person is not born autonomous. However, children have both the right and the natural tendency to develop their capacity for autonomy. If parents or educators don't create adequate space for the development of autonomy, it is an educational failure which often qualifies as neglect or indoctrination.[59]

These components of autonomy are commonly consensually accepted, although they don't occur systematically. However, a fundamental problem arises with a more detailed inspection. The definition is completely lacking the aspect of *extent* or *degree*. To what extent should an individual be free, rational competent, etc. to be characterized as autonomous? The vast majority of therapeutic educators are silent. Autonomy is simply postulated as a goal with no further description. Although this isn't explicitly stated, from specific didactic instructions it is clear that many theorists have in mind "complete" autonomy. See the recommendations by Raths, et al.—if children decide not to develop their moral values, that's their autonomous choice and the teacher must respect it.[60] A. S. Neill, founder of the *Summerhill School*, even went so far as to allow students, in the name of individual autonomy, to absent themselves from all classes if they so desired.[61] If Neill

---

57. Ibid.
58. Ibid., 119.
59. Haworth, *Autonomy*, 127.
60. Raths et al., *Values*, 41.
61. Neill, *Summerhill*, 29.

fought for freedom *in* school, Ivan Illich and other deschoolers advocated freedom *from* school, or absolute freedom.[62]

R. T. Allen connects this conception of autonomy with the existential emphasis of the time. At roughly the same time that therapeutic pedagogy praised autonomy as the final goal of (not only ethical) education, Jean Paul Sartre spoke of "complete" or "absolute" freedom as the mode of existance of human beings. In his conception, people are "self defining and self determining nothingness."[63] The question is, however, is this picture of humankind real? True? Pedagogically conceivable? The human I as a purely abstract concept, separate from any influence? Independent self-determination?

It is obvious that every instance of self determination requires self-knowledge, and that is not possible without situational grounding.[64] It seems that many pedocentrists forget that every man and woman had a childhood. Everyone is born into a specific environment—physical, social, moral, and so on,—and before beginning any reflecting or self determining, they acquire habits, bonds, relationships, community conditions, cultural patterns, inherited tendencies, language, concepts, opinions, convictions . . . In other words, people are beings who are "conditioned, situated and with a history."[65] If they choose (and are able) to distance themselves from any of their early "baggage," so be it. It is questionable to what extent they succeed, because it turns out that the material acquired in the initial phases of education are so deeply rooted in the psychic structure of an individual that it is very difficult to do anything with them later.[66] The point of the argument is clear—we are not as autonomous, independent, or unencumbered as we like to imagine. Neither as adults, nor as children. The concept of the "fully autonomous individual" is romantic, as well as, Allen adds, "incoherent, empty and unrealistic."[67]

Some liberal-therapeutic authors are aware of this problem, and try to qualify and make the concept more precise with the help of statements like "autonomous to a relatively high degree," or "in a relatively important

---

62. See texts such as Illich, *Deschooling.*

63. Allen, "Rational Autonomy," 201.

64. Cf. Page, "Entertaining," 109.

65. Allen, "Rational Autonomy," 205.

66. Cf. Thiessen, *Teaching*, 128.

67. Allen, "Rational Autonomy," 199–207.

respect."[68] But such formulations don't solve the problem, on the contrary, they raise it. To exactly what extent does a person need to be considered autonomous? Let us consider, for example, one of the above-mentioned components of autonomy—namely, the ability to make independent decisions on the basis of a good knowledge or awareness about the subject for decision. The fundamental question is, how much does an adult, let alone a child, need to know for it to be said they are informed enough to make a truly autonomous decision? For example, if they have to choose which worldview to hold, or whether to become a vegan, or what kind of spirituality to hold? It is not only impossible to get all the facts, even on an external, descriptive level, but children especially (and often adults too) do not have the ability to evaluate their reliability, conceive of their implications and consequences, or reflect on the consistency of the information, etc. If children are put into a situation in which they must decide for themselves, the one who put them there has acted extremely irresponsibly. Obviously, I am not thinking about trivial decisions such as whether to have a sandwich with cheese or with ham.

There is also another factor that is usually not considered. If you, for example, allow a child to choose from three activity groups, they often don't choose any of them because a) they quite frankly still don't know what they want, what they might want, what they enjoy or what they might enjoy; b) they might simply be lazy. Only when their parents—completely inadequately, in the judgment of the therapeutists—"force" them by saying something like "come on, let's try swimming and we'll see," i.e., they decide for the children, it can happen that the children discover they not only enjoy swimming, but they even have a talent for it. But that possibility would never develop if a liberal educator, armed with the doctrine of autonomy, left the decision to an immature child.

As far as moral values are concerned, this transfer of the responsibility for decision making is more than problematic. It's not only because children cannot know what is worthwhile, for the excellent reason that they are children. But also for the overlooked fact that we acquire the vast majority of all our opinions, convictions, and values not cognitively, that is, on the basis of rational reflection and consequent decisions, but on a relational, affective, social, communal, or even aesthetic level. I accept the view of the world of someone I know, someone I trust, someone I have experienced something with, or whom I love. Therefore, to want a child to make an

68. Deardon, "Autonomy," 458; Haydon, "Autonomy," 220.

intelligent, informed, autonomous choice at an age when they are incapable of doing so means, at best, throwing them into confusion, and at worst, raising a little tyrant.

And here is one more observation to conclude the problem of autonomy. How does the therapeutic philosophy of education deal with the possibility that someone, completely voluntarily and freely, gives up their freedom? Someone who submits or surrenders their life to some other person, idea, or mission. For example, a young athlete dedicating himself to a famous idol, or an ecologist to rescuing a dying species, a believer to God, a vegan to their guru, or a woman to her husband (or vice versa). Advocates of autonomous education usually argue that such individuals could not be qualified as autonomous, even though their decision was made autonomously. Irving Thalburg, for example—in the beautiful liberation years of the 1970s—claimed that women who voluntarily accept a submissive position cannot "be even faintly autonomous in their thinking or behavior," and that such submission is merely the result of "early indoctrination" or some other kind of "brainwashing." It is interesting to listen to the solution, or, literally "forcible re-education," that Thalburg suggests in such a case. An adult woman would need to go through a "new program of conditioning"—yes, such ideas prevailed in the then behavioral faith in the power of external manipulation of a person: we will simply re-code her. C. S. Lewis was right when predicting the "Cast of Conditioners" who will treat human beings as things (see the previous subsection, The "Abolition of Man"). Thalburg concludes that care must be taken that women be trained to hold autonomy as a conscious value from earliest childhood.[69]

This raises the question—are women (ecologists, athletes, or vegans) who are trained from childhood to treasure autonomy, truly autonomous? If their choice to hold as certain some specific value was conditioned, in what sense is that choice free or authentic? In other words, Thalburg's

---

69. Thalburg, "Socialization," 27, 29, 35–36. At this point I recall a conversation between Éowyn, the daughter of Rohan, and Theodene, the niece of the almost-king Aragorn, just before the Battle of Gondor, in which J. R. R. Tolkien uniquely expressed both an understanding of the need for human (not only feminine) autonomy, and his completely non-stereotypical view of human possibilities in this regard:

Éowyn: "Lord, if you must go, then let me ride in you following. For I am weary of skulking in the hills..."

Aragorn: "Your duty is with your people."

Éowyn: "Too often have I heard of duty," she cried. "But am I not of the House of Eorl, a shildmaiden . . . may I not spend my life as I will?"

Aragorn: "Few may do that with honour."

argument suffers from the same autoreferential blindness as the argument regarding indoctrination in the preceding chapter. When someone is conditioned to a different value than ours, it's indoctrination or brainwashing. When we condition them to our values, it's okay.

It is obviously necessary to find a better definition for autonomy. Let's see what the pedagogy of character offers.

The Method of Forming Character as a Reaction to "Therapy"

At the turn of the 1980s to the 1990s, criticism of the liberal-therapeutic approach to moral education took on the form of a real alternative. The criticism came from various sides—conservative, neohumanistic, neoclassical, and even feminist. Not every critic offered a positive pedagogical alternative, but some did, as we shall see. The common denominator of the criticism was the belief that a society which emphasizes the personal rights of the individual, but doesn't put the same emphasis on the binding nature of all specified and publicly-shared responsibilities, is untenable in the long run. The good of the individual is nonsense in the long term without the good of the whole. And a functional whole, that is, the social space in which it's possible to live (well) is not a matter of course, but something that requires effort on the part of its members. Efforts that are typical of moral competence go beyond the borders of personal interests in favor of common interests or the public good.

Furthermore, critics of the "therapeutists" are in agreement that the content side of moral or ethical education must be formulated and defended much more intensively than therapeutic pedagogy has admitted. The critics have also made it clear that there is no such thing as value neutrality. Everyone has some set of values arranged in a more or less well thought out hierarchy. Even those who claim that no real values exist, or that they are relative, are postulating a value statement such as, for example, "it should not be said that something is objectively valuable." A position of absolute relativism is dubious from at least three perspectives: 1) linguistically, it is an oxymoron, 2) logically, it suffers from an auto-referential inconsistency—because it refutes what it postulates, 3) above all it makes everyday interpersonal interaction meaningless. For example, advocates of absolute relativism expect others to tolerate their opinions, yet tolerance is a very non-relative value. Christina Hoff Sommers, one of the personalities in character education, asks whether we can say that "moral knowledge" really exists. She goes on to answer that if we've learned anything from the last millenium of civilization, we have to say yes; to say we don't know about grace, human rights, and virtues would be only foolish pretending. It's obvious that things like arbitrary cruelty, and political oppression are wrong, and that kindness and political freedom are right and good. If we don't pass on our moral traditions to the next generation we'll be the first society in history to thus hamstring itself.[70]

Michael Horowitz says something similar when he expresses the nature of the emerging pedagogical emphasis—"the pendulum is swinging back from self-expression to self discipline."[71] From this critical range of views came an educational philosophy, or tradition, promoting an emphasis on character formation. It stands on several basic principles that I will attempt to outline.

Metaphysical Realism

Character educators are openly calling for the traditional concept of education that preceded the pedocentric and therapeutic turn-arounds. Moral cosmology is founded on so-called metaphysical realism, which basically expresses the following: the nature of the world (the cosmos, including human beings) is an objective reality whose complexity is not accidental or without meaning, but on the contrary is imbued with meaning and knowable. The order of the universe is made known to us through all of our cognitive capacities—rational, emotional, aesthetic, spiritual, etc. This also applies to ethical reality—every civilization and culture in history has touched, formulated, and preserved this reality in one way or another. They may differ in their ways of expressing and justifying this reality, they may also differ in the degree of consistency with which they uphold this moral reality, but they all agree that it exists and must be respected. There are cultures which, for example, train their offspring to revere their parents (sometimes even the dead ones), and others that preach the honoring of the offspring, but there is no culture that doesn't revere anything. Else it wouldn't be a human culture. We also recognize that the quality of the object of reverence determines the quality of the culture. Therefore it is necessary to maintain a continual reflection on the culture—figuratively speaking, to examine what we worship and why.

70. Sommers, "Teaching."
71. In Fineman, "Virtuecrats," 36.

From this historical experience flows the principle of the universally-shared law which is understood as *natural*, meaning that it is part of both the nature of the world and the nature of human beings, and between the two natures there prevails a "pre-ordained harmony."[72] Different authors have called it different names. C. S. Lewis calls it "Tao," deliberately suggesting that moral laws are equally accessible to both the West and the East.[73] Teachers of character speak of "core morality," the "moral canon" and "universal law."[74] Good and evil are not a matter of opinion, but express qualities of reality which humanity recognizes across space and time. The reality of the moral law is confirmed by experience—keeping it leads to the good of the individual and the whole, violating it leads to the decay of society.

Because humanity—according to the teachers of character—is not born complete or finished, the only way they can acquire moral laws, values, and virtues is through education, the process of character formation. This process aims at not only developing moral reflexes or judgments but also cultivating moral behavior and moral convictions. A natural part of this process is leading the student towards respect for authority, whether institutional or personal, as well as an appropriate system of rewards and punishment.

The Teaching of Habits and Teaching by Habit

One of the didactic pillars of the pedagogy of character stands on Aristotle's timeless observation that virtue is acquired the same as any other human skill—through action and practice, through virtuous behavior. Let the famous passage from his *Nicomachean Ethics* be heard:

> But the virtues we get by first exercising them, as also happens in the case of the arts as well. For the things we have to learn before we can do them, we learn by doing them, e.g. men become builders by building and lyreplayers by playing the lyre; so too we become just by doing just acts, temperate by doing temperate acts, brave by doing brave acts.[75]

Inspired by Aristotle, most character educators believe that there is a natural potential for virtue within human nature—an innate tendency

---

72. Lewis, *Pilgrim's Regress*, 169.

73. Lewis, *Abolition of Man*, 29.

74. Cf. Hunter, *Death*, 108.

75. Aristotle, *Nicomachean Ethics*, 1.

towards temperance, fairness, bravery, etc. Nevertheless, without properly getting used to virtuous behavior, virtue is never achieved. It remains only on the level of potential, sometimes on the level of theory—people know about it, sometimes even see it in someone else, but are not capable of it themselves, simply because no one ever led them to try it, to experience it, or to get used to it so it became natural. In order for it to become one's nature, it is necessary to repeatedly do it. Thomas Lickona bases the goals of the pedagogy of character on this principle: "Good character consists of knowing the good, desiring good, and doing good—habits of the mind, habits of the heart, and habits of actions."[76]

Educators of character recognize, along with Aristotle, that the formation of virtuous habits is only the foundation or start of a much wider process of initiation into the art of virtue. Virtuous people do not merely act according to habit without thinking, but they can differentiate between various moral goals, purposes, and situations on both the cognitive and affective levels. Moral habits only prepare the ground for the development of the kind of moral behavior that the individual does with intent, not mindlessly. The process of initiation, however, cannot happen without an initiator, an educator, parent, or teacher. As the process of socialization requires a socializer. Because this is an initiation into virtue, the teacher must be virtuous. Otherwise it simply won't work. "Just as in art," explains Aristotle, "It is from the same causes and by the same means that every virtue is produced . . . , it is from playing the lyre that both good and bad lyre-players are produced . . . If this were not so, there would have been no need of a teacher."[77] Thus the teacher is definitely not perceived as merely an assistant to the moral self-development of the child, but as an essential agent who initiates the cultivation of moral habits, introduces ways of moral thinking and consciously leads the child to moral behavior. Socrates would probably agree, but he would ask (not only Aristotle) whether he knew any virtuous teachers.

Story and Meta-story as a Didactic Tool

That the story has the unique power to pass along moral content and influence the affective component of personality is universally well known. Likewise, that there can be no story without a meta-story. That is why

76. Lickona, *Educating*, 51.

77. Aristotle, *Nicomachean Ethics*, 1.

therapeutic educators did not indulge in the narrative form of teaching very much. They didn't want to "submit" to any pre-given ethical metanarrative, which stories necessarily contain. For the exact same reason, the teachers of character have always loved, encouraged, and enjoyed stories as didactic tools. It comes from the fact that all legends, dramas, epics, and fairy tales passed down from generation to generation contain a robust moral heritage which has the power to both strengthen desirable moral behavior, and stigmatize undesirable behavior. William J. Bennett explains his intention frankly: "Many of the clearest moral lessons can be found in the classic stories from literature and history."[78] And elsewhere he adds the concise fact that "children enjoy stories."[79] Similarly, Gary Bauer does not question the "great educational strength of the story . . . , the literary tool which shows rather than explains" the shoulds and shouldn'ts.[80] And one more example out of many others, Christine Sommers is convinced that "helping children become acquainted with their moral heritage in literature, in religion, and in philosophy is a universally stablished way to teach the virtues."[81]

Proponents of the pedagogy of character also offer psychological reasons for using stories in ethical education. It comes from the observation that human thought operates in at least two different modes—propositional and narrative. Both kinds of thinking organize and structure human experience, but each in a completely different way; they cannot be interchanged or replaced. The propositional mode operates on the level of concepts and logic, which is in principle independent of all emotional, social, historic, and other contexts. For example, a statement of the type "If $a > b$ and $b > c$, then $a > c$" really is not too emotionally charged (for most normal people), however true and useful it is. On the other hand, the narrative mode requires not only thinking, but also calls for imagination, emotional engagement, the distinguishing of contexts, specifics of place and time, the intentions of the narrator, etc. Therefore, morally tuned skills such as empathy cannot in fact be generated, or even held, merely on the basis of some abstract logical principle. On the other hand, the narrative mode has this very power. The reader or listener to a story "engages" in a variety of ways, it pulls in their own storylines, stresses, makes them think, gives the opportunity to identify with characters, but also the structure of the narrative

---

78. Bennett, *Book of Virtue*, 16.
79. Ibid., 16.
80. Bauer, "The Moral," 26.
81. Sommers, "Teaching," 13.

or narrator enables word play, etc. Moreover, all of this affects the reader or listener organically, as a whole, which is clearly the main reason for the didactic effectiveness of stories. "So just as a person isn't only a rational being but is also emotional and physical, etc., neither does a story work in isolation, only in the mind, or only in the emotions, etc. A person exposed to the power of story is a being who goes through a holistic experience in which she thinks, feels, believes, endures, identifies with, receives information, evaluates, etc."[82] Hence the enjoyment of narrative forms by teachers of character.

The formative power of a story was eventually also recognized by the more liberal spectrum of approaches to ethical education. Soon after Bennet published his famous *Book of Virtue*, Colin Greer and Herbert Kohl published a similar compendium entitled *A Call to Character: A Family Treasury of Stories, Poems, Plays, Proverbs and Fables to Guide the Development of Values for You and Your Children*. Apart from the fact that the book was compiled with a decidedly liberal-therapeutic intent, it brought a little terminological confusion into the discussion. That is because the title contains the key word "character," which is normally associated with their opponents' pedagogy. It's possible that that was the intention. In publishing the book the authors admitted that the "subjugation" of moral content, or "indoctrination" as they understood it, is unavoidable, but they also bring a fundamental question into the discussion. When a story must be told that will anchor the child in some moral tradition, whose story will it be? Or whose tradition? Likewise, in what metanarrative framework do we tell the components of didactic stories? And to what kind of morality are we directing them? Conservative? Liberal? Mormon, Islamic, Communist, or Martian (yes, there are institutions which programmatically care about the rights of extraterrestrial civilizations)? In other words—it's necessary to re-emphasize the fact that no story is value neutral, neither small individual stories nor grand metanarratives. It also needs to be said that just as there are good and bad stories (Hamlet vs. Rambo), there are also good and bad meta-stories in the sense of ethics, and we need to have an honest dialogue and apparently never-ending battle over the *truth* of our metanarratives and cultural traditions. I emphasize the epistomologically and philosophically difficult word *truth*. The search for truthfulness (in anything) has always been difficult, but from the perspective of ethical education it is indispensable, because refusing to join that search is immoral.

82. Hábl, *Teaching*, 57.

This can be seen clearly in the current, politically correct but shallow concept of tolerance, which—in captivity to the ideology of multicultural-ism—claims that all traditions and cultures are the same and we may not judge them in any way.[83] Such tolerance is 1) completely naïve, because it is uninformed about the facts—such as that the ethical culture of the Amish is truly different than that of the Mahayana Buddhists; 2) pedagogically it is utterly helpless when confronted with the meta-ethical questions raised by the students. For example, the story Kim Jong-il (or Jong-un) tells to his pupils is different than the one told by Mother Theresa, and both are differ-ent than the one told by a radical Imam. Each one has a different content, form and implication. When a child asks the philosophical meta-question, which of those meta-stories is better or more truthful, whatever the teacher answers one thing is certain—if they say they're all the same, it is immoral.

Teaching and Learning Community

The importance of community, or social environment, for education is generally known. Pedagogues from both camps recognize and develop it in their educational programs. Kohlberg, for example, repeatedly talks about the need for cultivating a "just community" and "civic education." Lickona warns that "character does not exist in a vacuum" but in a social space, and therefore institutions (not only schools) must be intentionally "caring com-munities." However, therapeutic teachers and teachers of character differ in the nature of the educational "care," or methods used in one or the other's educational community.

Critics of the therapeutic method point to the fact that the pro-community rhetoric contrasts both with the individualistic philosophy of education on which it is based, and the individualistic results of education which this method unsurprisingly brings. If Kohlberg defines his concept of a "just community" as a community in which "democratic participa-tion structures moral judgements, decision-making, and action," then he is defining the basic problem.[84] Education is a dynamic process composed of diverse events, situations, and circumstances which often don't allow "democratic" participation. If participation is dogmatically applied it cre-ates the problem that it was originally intended to solve—it produces moral individuals who have been taught that moral principles are not respected

83. For more on this issue see Danišková, "Marx."

84. Power, et al., "Democratic Schools," 26.

at all, but negotiated and sometimes self-determined. In other words, I can go as far as others allow me to. Not every therapeutic school is as dogmatic in this respect, but it shows the logical proportions: the more dogmatic the emphasis on individual self-determination, the more individualistic—and potentially socially-conflictive—is the individual produced.

When teachers of character talk about a community that could provide educational potential, they don't think of it as a sum of individuals, but as an "organic body" in which people are mutually and intersubjectively connected by a common vision, beliefs, goals, etc.[85] As with an individual, a community has character, and the character of the community influences the character of its individuals. How? Much has already been written about this by the sociologists and social psychologists, so here I will write only briefly. A community has its history, events, drama, and experiences which have formed it—it has its own story. The members of a community become both participants and co-authors of that story. Each community also has its norms, doctrines, and beliefs, as well as rewards and sanctions. In addition, they have a moral language that relates to moral reality, along with their own specific rituals, customs, symbols, hierarchy, etc. Within this the individuals are formed, positively and negatively. Lickona gives examples from his clinical studies which document how immorality in the social environment does, in fact, lead to immoral behavior among its members.[86] Respondents from selected locations (in New York) knew what they "should" do, but answered that "here" it would be "foolish." There is no need to explain that it also functions oppositely—in a society which has a highly cultivated morality, immorality appears foolish.

Aware of the influence of the external environment on the individual, teachers of character emphasize two educational principles: a) formation of virtue is not only an individual, but also a social, or "civic" matter, says Hunter;[87] b) educational institutions must consciously work on being the kind of communities in which virtuous behavior is easy and natural.

Holistic Emphasis

Formation of character does not only concern moral reasoning, that is, the development of the rational capacity of the individual, but every capacity,

---

85. Dykstra, *Vision*, 55.
86. Lickona, *Educating*, 63.
87. Hunter, *Death*, 112.

and thus, the whole person. An emphasis on integrity is clear from the way we understand *good* character. Lickona defines three components: good character includes "knowing what is good, feeling what is good, doing what is good—habits of the mind, heart, and behavior."[88] Individuals with good character are able to judge what is right, be interested in what is right, and also do what they believe is right. Lickona accompanies the components with a diagram that highlights their interdependence and integrity. Moral knowledge can foster the emergence and development of moral feelings, moral feelings shape moral judgments and behavior, and all the components influence each other—our behavior affects our thoughts and our feelings. Aggressive acts can awaken aggressive thoughts and emotions, and on the contrary, kind acts can awaken kind emotions.

Figure 1

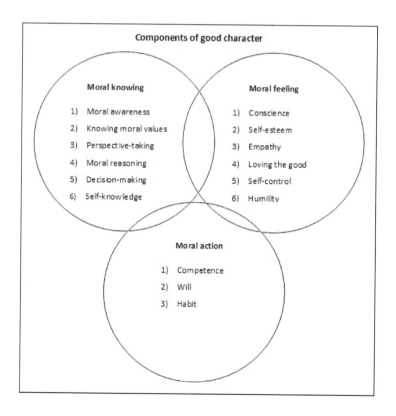

88. Lickona, *Educating*, 51.

Moral Knowledge

As shown in the diagram, Lickona distinguishes six kinds of moral knowledge:

1. *Moral awareness.* It is a basic knowledge of rules and norms. What is right and what is not.

2. *Knowledge of moral values.* Lickona does not define all individual values, he only lists the ones he considers as a "moral heritage one generation passes on to the next"—freedom, responsibility, honesty, integrity, etc. Lickona gives special attention to the two values that express the fundamental relationship between individuals and society: *respect* (towards individuals) and *responsibility* (of the individual to the whole). The work of educators is to teach children to apply these values to specific situations.

3. *Perspective-taking or knowledge of points of view.* Once children have been safely anchored in their own moral traditions, they can be directed to also look at other traditions and perspectives. Moral maturity means that the individual has acquired the ability to see events and situations from the other person's perspective—whether culturally similar or completely differenet.

4. *Moral judgment.* At a certain stage in the development of reason, children begin to think conceptually, to understand, to judge, etc. In the area of morality it means that the individual will be led to an understanding of the reasons for moral behavior. Why it is good to behave morally, what it means to be moral, and so on.

5. *Moral decision-making.* The ability to decide presupposes rational reflection—of specific moral situations, specific possibilities, the consequences of deciding, and so on. A morally competent individual is able not only to judge, but also to decide.

6. *Moral self-knowledge.* Knowledge of oneself is one of the most difficult, says Lickona. Nevertheless, it is an important prerequisite for the development of character. The ability to explore your behavior, thoughts, and motives. Knowledge of your own strengths and weaknesses. The ability to admit unpleasant facts about your tendencies, etc.

Moral Feelings

1. *Conscience.* Lickona distinguishes two aspects of conscience—cognitive and emotional, i.e., on the one hand knowledge of what is good, and on the other a sense of commitment to act on that knowledge. Lickona does not analyze the reasons for that commitment, only stating that a mature conscience includes a sense of responsibility or commitment. People who behave according to their conscience experience positive (Lickona calls them "constructive") emotions, if they behave contrary to their conscience, they feel guilty.

2. *Self-esteem.* Awareness of one's own value and meaning is foundational to a healthy relationship with oneself. And a healthy relationship with oneself is foundational to healthy relationships with others. Studies show that individuals with a healthy degree of self-esteem are less dependent on the opinions of others, and therefore better able to resist peer pressure and other such influences. But the attribute "healthy" is key. How is a healthy sense of selfworth or self-esteem built? People base their evaluations on various more or less valuable commodities—appearance, property, popularity, performance, and so on. Lickona suggests building children's self-esteem on qualities such as honesty, diligence, courtesy, responsibility, etc.

3. *Empathy.* The ability to feel what another person is feeling is actually an emotional variant of the knowledge of points of view, mentioned above. Lickona qualifies the empathy that he is referring to with the attribute of "generalized," that is, one that corresponds to principles of humanity.

4. *Love of good.* Good character by nature loves good and abhors evil. Morally mature individuals find pleasure in doing good, good being more attractive to them than evil. For such people, the moral of *obligation* has grown into the moral of *desire* (for good). From the perspective of education this means that it is necessary to train not only the mind, but also the "heart."

5. *Self-control.* Sometimes the mind controls the emotions, other times the emotions overwhelm the mind. Sometimes the mind and the emotions overcome ordinary laziness or comfort. Thus, the necessity of the virtue of self-control, or self-denial, which enables people to behave morally even when they don't want to. This is a character quality

that cannot be taken for granted, it won't appear on its own. It must be systematically and consciously cultivated.

6. *Humility*. This is an affective component of self-knowledge that includes genuine openness to the truth and a readiness to admit and correct one's own failures. Humility is also the best protection against the temptation to behave badly. In this context Lickona cites Blaise Pascal, where he notes that "evil is never done so thoroughly or so well, as when it is done with a good conscience."[89] [/NL 1-6]

Lickona adds that putting the components of moral feelings together with the components of moral knowledge, creates a source of moral motivation. In fact, moral feelings "help us to cross the bridge from knowing what is right to doing it." The presence, or absence, of moral feelings in human character largely determines and explains why some people behave according to their moral principles and others do not. "For this reason," he continues, moral education "that is merely intellectual—that touches the mind but not the heart—misses a crucial part of character."[90]

Moral Behavior

The ability to act morally is, to a large extent, the result of the cultivation of the two preceding componenets of good character. People who have the qualities of moral knowledge and moral feelings will probably behave in accordance with that knowledge and those feelings. But it isn't automatic. It is a fact that as people we often know or feel what is good, and yet don't act accordingly. What is the driving force of character that leads a person to behave morally? Lickona presents three final components.

1. *Competence*. It is the capacity or skill to transfer moral knowledge and feelings into practical moral action. Later in his work Lickona elaborates on how to cultivate this competence educationally. Here he confines himself to stating only that there are many moral competencies (the art of listening, the art of communicating, etc.), and that they apply in everyday moral situations.

2. *Will*. Not only the right choice in moral situations, but the fundamental will to act on what I know and feel is right. We are now touching on

89. Lickona, *Educating*, 61.
90. Ibid.

perhaps the most difficult aspect of moral character. The will is necessary for self-control, control over emotions, tendencies and temptation to evil. The will is also needed to resist the pressure from a peer group or any majority that does not follow the moral goals. "Will is at the core of moral courage," Lickona concluded.[91]

3. *Habit.* The strength of habit is universally well-known—in both positive and negative senses. People who behave well, politely, honestly, courteously, etc., usually do so because (from childhood) they have been accustomed to doing so. Or they are simply used to it. If the phenomenon of habit is to serve good character, it is necessary from the earliest age to ensure the greatest number of opportunities to develop good habits and thereby avoid bad habits.

Lickona's classification of the components of character is to a certain extent arbitrary—as is, after all, any classification based on criteria chosen by a researcher. Some of the components overlap or duplicate each other (see, for example, self-control in area 2 and the will in area 3), some are missing, and it might be worth considering how to integrate them into Lickona's model (for example, the social, spiritual, etc. components). Nevertheless, it is a reasonable attempt to deal with moral character systematically and honestly. Lickona clearly states his holistic emphasis—morality is not only a cognitive question, but also pertains to other aspects of one's personality. Every aspect is mutually connected, thereby creating a complete unity. Effective moral education must, therefore, be effective in all the previously mentioned componenets of personality—cognitive, emotional, and behavioral.

Non-indoctrinating Indoctrination

We have already touched on the problem of indoctrination. It is such a large and important chapter in (not only moral) education, that I want to now give it some special attention. Who would want to be accused of the capital pedagogical sin of indoctrination? It is a pejorative concept, and we have seen that therapeutic educators have strictly dismissed traditional moral education as merely indoctrination. However, teachers of character, who have often been reported as taking the traditional approach, object, saying that if indoctrination were defined then even therapeutic education

91. Ibid., 62.

would not be immune. This raises two fundamental questions that will be the subject of this subchapter: a) what exactly does it mean to indoctrinate? b) is education without indoctrination even possible?

As far as the definition is concerned, Elmer J. Thiessen has clearly and most thoroughly discussed this phenomenon in his book *Teaching for Commitment*, where he reacts to the terminological chaos surrounding the word. Thiessen's approach is unique in that he does not present any kind of abstract conceptual analysis of the term, but pays careful attention to everyone who has treated the concept of indoctrination, synthesizing the partial objections into a coherent form, so that it is clear what exactly makes indoctrination, indoctrination. He then applies those facts to specific educational approaches, both traditional and liberal.[92] Thiessen's contribution is very relevant to the theme of this book, therefore in the following paragraphs I will briefly outline it, contrasting it with other authors from various ideological camps.

Thiessen identifies four or five criteria or areas in which indoctrination can occur: i) content, ii) method(s), iii) intention, iv) effects, v) some educational theorists would also add institutional as a criterium, in the sense that some educational institutions are, or necessarily must be, *a priori* indoctrinational because of the nature of what they are.

Content

In the first place, indoctrination is associated with a certain kind of content. Certain doctrines or systems of doctrine form a specific worldview or ideology. Terms like doctrine and ideology have their own pejorative connotations, but in the twilight of modernity (the second half of the twentieth century) they were mainly connected with politics and religion. The only discourse considered to be free of any doctrine was scientific discourse, because it is supposedly based only "on pure facts, rationality, rigorous logic and objective experience."[93] When the word doctrine was used

---

92. The practicality and functionality of Thiessen's methodological approach is evident in the kind of language he uses in the Introduction to illustrate his goal: If a town decree says that no "means of transport" are allowed in the park and someone asks whether a skateboard is a means of transport, it isn't necessary to formulate a deep and complex definition of what is and is not a "means of transport," but just to deal with the question directly, that is, to ask whether we want to allow skateboarding in the park or not (cf. Thiessen, *Teaching*, 31).

93. Cf. Kazepides, "Indoctrination"; Barrow and Woods, *Philosophy*; Hirst, *Knowledge*.

it was always understood to mean "unscientific," (and thus) "erroneous," "irrational," "ideological," "dogmatic," etc. This exclusive status of science has today, of course, been lost. The current scientific community, for the most part, no longer holds the romantic ideal of "scientific quality," because it is aware that the distance between the knower and the object known is not as unproblematic as modernity thought. Every scientist has a certain pre-understanding, a set of doctrines, theories, and principles which are nonnegotiable, yet which determine the human understanding of reality. Nevertheless, the discussion about indoctrination has its roots in the height of the period of modernity, and its spirit lives on. If you ask a modern romantic (liberal scientific educator) which doctrines (content) trigger indoctrination, here is a summary:

a. *Faulty doctrines.* Simply wrong, not based on the facts. Wilson calls these doctrines "irrational."[94]

b. *Unsupported or insufficiently substantiated doctrines.* What underpins doctrines, is evidence. An unsupported doctrine is questionable, dubious, uncertain, vague, or—as Wilson says—lacking "publicly accepted evidence."[95]

c. *Doctrines which cannot be confirmed or refuted.* The anti-indoctrinational ideal of twentieth-century liberal educational theorists has a direct connection with the positivist principle, verification-falsification. It says that any statement or doctrine that cannot be confirmed by the scientific method is de facto insignificant, because there is no existing criteria by which it is possible to judge its truthfulness or falsity. Moral, aesthetic, and religious statements thus fall into this category, because they are not scientifically evaluable. Anyone who would teach them would inevitably indoctrinate. There is a consensus among the therapeutists on this subject.[96]

d. *Ideological doctrines.* Flew, in one of his arguments, recognizes that not every belief that people hold must necessarily represent a doctrine which eventually becomes the subject of indoctrination. If human conviction is to "degenerate" into doctrine, it must be "tied to

---

94. Wilson, "Freedom," 103.

95. Wilson, "Education," 28.

96. See Kazepides, "Indoctrination," 235; Flew, "Doctrines," 78; Snook, *Indoctrination*, 33; White, "Indoctrination," 192; Gregory and Woods, "Indoctrination," 173.

something broad and ideological," says Flew.[97] He doesn't give any concrete examples, but I think that he has in mind that doctrines, as opposed to partial statements or convictions, are elements of some universally-explanatory metanarrative or overall philosophy of life.

e. *Engaging doctrines.* It bothers the resisters of doctrine that their acceptance "is no mere academic matter—there is commitment to act in particular ways, to profess and act out a particular value and way of life."[98] Wilson cautions that political and moral doctrines have a tendency to be "closer to the heart of an individual than other beliefs."[99] It's no wonder that "doctrines have a primarily prescriptive function," states Kazepides, i.e., they are engaging, and cause people to live according to them.[100]

f. *Doctrines propagated with enthusiasm.* Resisters of doctrine are further bothered that those on whom some doctrine "falls," have a tendency to hold onto that doctrine and propagate it with all their might and enthusiasm.[101] Gregory and Woods clarify that this is because holders of doctrines consider them to be of momentous concern for mankind, and that is why it further leads them to "a strong urge to convince others, the waverers, the unbelievers, of their essential truth."[102] If all the preceding characteristics of doctrine describe the status of doctrines, or sometimes what the doctrines cause (see the previous paragraph), this one tries to express how they are handled by those who hold them.

g. *Institutionally supported doctrines.* This final characteristic is related to the previous one. Because doctrines are perceived as fundamentally important, they have a tendency to become institutionalized. Some communities, organizations, or institutions can grab hold of them, protect them, care for them, and proclaim them. Kazepides says that doctrines necessarily "presuppose the existence of authorities or institutions which have the power to uphold them when they

---

97. Flew, "Doctrines," 71.
98. Gregory and Woods, "Indoctrination," 166.
99. Wilson, "Education," 27.
100. Kazepides, "Indoctrination," 35.
101. Cf. Scruton et al., *Education*, 24.
102. Gregory and Woods, "Indoctrination," 168.

are challenged by critics, heretics, or the faithless, and punish the enemies."[103] In this sense Flew, and Gregory and Woods, often cite the Roman Catholic Church or the Communist Party as examples of contexts from which this undesireable doctrinality could come.[104]

How do supporters of character education respond? Thiessen first points to the fact that there is no definition for the concept of doctrine. The critics of doctrines evidently regard the whole question of doctrinality as dubious and suspicious, but never offer any definition of exactly what a doctrine is.

All the other critical responses point to one common denominator—the problem of self-referencing, which has already been mentioned several times. It is a simple, but not trivial criterion for judging the meaningfulness of thought systems—any statement, system of statements, or methodological principle that claims to be true must withstand the self-referential test, i.e., it must apply even when it refers to itself. When someone makes a statement like "I can't speak a word of English," it is obviously false because the content denies the message. It's the same with the central doctrine of the positivist concept to which the therapeutists refer. It claims that *only what is empirically verifiable, is true.* The problem with the statement is that it is not empirically verifiable. It suffers from the same self-referential inconsistency. The same can be seen in all the above-mentioned criteria of content—the critics have forgotten to apply them to themselves. What version of therapeutic education does not hold its own (content) doctrines about people, the world, truth, the meaning of being, morality, etc? Do not liberal thinkers regard their liberal values as meaningful, or morally important? Don't they espouse them with unflagging enthusiasm? Aren't they committed to (engaged in) their cause? Don't they even have institutions behind them which make sure the liberal model is spread, promoted, and taught? Isn't the liberal concept of morality part of a broader worldview as well as political regime? Could we not, after all, speak of liberal ideology—and not only in the educational sense?

One more example for everyone. Therapeutists think that indoctrination occurs when doctrines are taught which do not have the attribute of general consensus or public agreement. The question arises—do the liberal doctrines have that consensus? What do "general" and "public" mean in

103. Kazepides, "Indoctrination," 235.

104. Flew, "Doctrines," 75–76, 79; Flew, "Religion," 106, 109; Gregory and Woods, "Indoctrination," 166, 187–88.

this context? One hundred percent agreement by the public? Or only by the experts? Either way, the therapeutists evidently don't have it, and thus they indoctrinate. The thief is shouting "Catch the thief!" This is the point of the whole argument on the criteria of content. Liberal therapeutic education maintains its specific (provincial and period) doctrines (of content) just as every other philosophy of education does, but would like to be protected by science, universality, or the public so it can claim that it is the only one that is right, the only one that educates while all the others indoctrinate.

To avoid any misunderstanding, that conclusion does not imply that in the end everyone indoctrinates, nor vice versa, that indoctrination doesn't exist. I am merely stating that the liberal definition of the criteria of content is so vague that it also applies to the liberals themselves. Everyone who teaches, conveys doctrines. And those doctrines can be true or false. The black-and-white vision of the liberal theorists of eduation—true content from us, false from them, *ergo* proper education with us, indoctrination with them—is untenable. And to make it even more difficult for liberal educators, we will see in the following chapter that it is possible to impart completely truthful content while indoctrinating, because pedagogical intent, aims, strategies, and other factors also come into play. In other words, it is possible to indoctrinate to the truth, but also to the opposite: it is possible, with very good and honest didactics, to lead someone into error.

Methodology

Every educator intuitively knows that in education, the method by which content is conveyed is just as important as the content itself. Thus, it's not only *what* is taught, but *how* it is taught. Methods can be good or bad. It is therefore necessary to pose the question: What makes a method bad, or in our case, indoctrinating? Here are some characteristics:

a. *Lack of evidence.* This problem can have at least four different nuances. 1) Methods which simply do not provide enough reasons, proofs, or arguments for the material being taught. Hull says, "reasons are concealed and reason is bypassed."[105] 2) Methods which place the question *what* over the question *how*. To this Green adds that "when, in teaching, we are concerned simply to lead another person to a correct answer, but are not correspondingly concerned that they arrive at the answer

---

105. Hull, *Studies*, 178.

on the basis of good reasons, then we are indoctrinating."[106] 3) Methods based on "mindless drill, recitation and rote memorization."[107] 4) Methods which force, which persuade individuals "by force of the indoctrinator's personality, by emotional appeal, or by use of a variety of rhetorical devices," rather than by reasons, evidence, and proof.[108]

b. *Misuse of evidence.* The misuse can occur in several ways: 1) Direct falsification or fraud. 2) Rationalization of the evidence in the sense that what is inconclusive is presented as if it were conclusive.[109] 3) Manipulation of the reasons in order to confirm the given conclusion. Rationality here does not serve truth, but self-confirms or defends one's own position.[110] 4) "A one-sided or biased presentation of a debatable issue," and sometimes "suppression of counter-evidence."[111] 5) The evidence can be misused in controversial issues, but also in common ones. Crittenden cautions that indoctrination occurs whenever "the criteria of inquiry" are violated.[112] 6) Flew states that indoctrination also occurs when the "logical status" of the doctrines being taught is violated, that is, when beliefs which are not true, or at least are not known to be true, are taught as if they are true.[113]

c. *Abuse of the teacher-student relationship.* 1) The authoritarian approach. Teachers and instructors are on principle in the position of authority, but if they misuse that authority it is authoritarianism, which is unacceptable and inevitably implies indoctrination.[114] 2) Threat to student autonomy. This directly relates to the previous problem. The authoritarian teacher suppresses the students' freedom. Autonomy is, like authority, a matter of degree. To what degree should autonomy be allowed without the teacher falling into indoctrination? This is difficult to define on a general level, but there is a consensus that a limit does exist, beyond which it's possible to say that a teacher fails to re-

---

106. Green, "Beliefs," 37.
107. Passmore, "Teaching," 193.
108. Benson, "Forms," 336.
109. Cf. Wilson, "Freedom," 19, 21.
110. Thiessen, *Teaching*, 89.
111. Moore, "Democratic method," 93.
112. Crittenden, "Mis-education," 146.
113. Flew, "Doctrines," 75–76.
114. Cf. Ibid., 47–48.

spect the individual's freedom, and thus indoctrinates.[115] 3) Dogmatic approach. If a teacher promotes "the misleading impression that p is true because [he] says it is," he indoctrinates, notes Benson.[116] And Crittenden adds that a dogmatic approach does not allow the learner "to examine voluntarily, to raise questions and objections and so on."[117] 4) Rewards and punishments. Green believes that the use of rewards and punishments may cause students "to learn to respond correctly or without hesitation," but not on the basis of evidence but in expectation of reward or punishment.[118]

d. *Neglect of intellectual virtues.* This is Arisotle's term to express the kind of qualities needed in the search for truth. Such intellectual qualities include the desire for evidence, objectivity, consistency of thought and integrity, courage to rethink one's view, argumentational rigor, etc. Spiecker[119] and Passmore,[120] as well as many others, consider the development of these virtues in children to be a necessary prerequisite to critical thinking. On the other hand, methods which don't favor these are considered to be indoctrinational.[121]

e. *Non-rationality.* All the methods mentioned above have one feature in common: "inculcating beliefs by the use of non-rational methods."[122] The methods are non-rational in that they (summarizing everything preceding): either manipulate the material by not securing proper evidence, or manipulate the students so they don't acquire knowledge independently, freely, and rationally, but on the basis of authority, emotions, or rewards and punishments.

It appears that the liberal theoreticians of education have succeeded, with the help of methodological criteria, in defining the border between indoctrinating and non-indoctrinating approaches. But there are some seriously interconnected problems which call for a closer look. First, let's look at the basic requirement of all methodological approaches, rationality.

---

115. Cf. Peters, *Authority*, 155.
116. Benson, "Forms," 336–37.
117. Crittenden, "Mis-education," 139.
118. Green, "Beliefs," 35.
119. Spiecker, "Indoctrination."
120. Passmore, "Teaching."
121. Cf. Moore, "Indoctrination," 98.
122. Spiecker, "Indoctrination," 262.

Almost still in the spirit of Enlightenment reductionism, children should be led only by rational methods to themselves become rational, critically thinking, independent persons who are capable of evaluating evidence, distinguishing fact from opinion, etc. I don't want to get bogged down in the complexities of epistemological issues regarding the possibilities of human reason, but I must raise one question. How are the children to acquire these rational skills and qualities? The problem—for the liberal theoreticians—is that this kind of acquisition doesn't necessarily happen on a rational level, especially in the initial stages of human life. When children are born they find themselves in a completely non-autonomous and authoritative situation. Parents, teachers, and society have determined the cultural, moral, and intellectual heritage into which the children are placed. The children are simply in no position to vote. Values, patterns, models, etc. are taken on primarily by habit, imitation, and identification, which are all non-rational processes. In order to avoid misunderstandings, we must first distinguish between the *subject* of habits (imitation and identification), and the *mechanism* of these processes. The subject, that which is imitated, can be completely understandable and rational, but the mechanism of imitation is a process that does not necessarily include a rational element. Children learn to be rational by imitating rational examples, even though the process of imitation is not a rational one. The foundation of rationality is thus, paradoxically, not formed in a rational way. A girl seeing her mother cooking and wanting her own kitchen has nothing to do with reason. The way parents help their children to clean their teeth is not with evidence and rational arguments (they come later, when the child is able to understand them), but with a cute little toothbrush. We don't allow a discussion—to the liberal theoreticians this smacks of authoritarianism—but simply, teeth must be cleaned, toys must not be broken, and fingers must not be sucked. They will understand why, later.

It is only after a child's initiation into a specific tradition that the didactic stage of questioning or critical evaluation of that tradition can come. From the educational standpoint, however, the crucial thing is what happens in the critical period when the child is subordinate to authority. Critics might argue here that this is well-known, and that the above discussion on indoctrination does not concern the early stage of education. But that is a mistake—if indoctrination happens in situations of confrontation with authority, then it is precisely in the early phase that it is essential to distinguish acceptable (educational) methods from unacceptable (indoctrinational) methods. And it is here that we can see the problem with the liberal definition—if "acceptable" for a method means purely rational, then every initiation is necessarily indoctrination. Once again, the liberal definition fails the self-reference test. The point of the argument, though, is that it is a mistake to call educational initiation, indoctrination. This is implied by the liberal definition, but that only shows that the definition is wrong.

Intention or Goals

It has already been said that the primary intent, or final goal, of therapeutic education is *autonomy*. The teacher or instructor who "deliberately intends to hinder the growth of a student towards autonomy, indoctrinates," says Hare.[123] McLaughlin similarly finds that indoctrination "constitutes an attempt to restrict in a substantial way the child's eventual ability to function autonomously."[124] For the sake of order, I will remind the reader of the pillars of the liberal therapeutic ideal of autonomy:

1. *Freedom.* An autonomous individual is free, and free (in this context) usually means "the absence of constraints or restraints relevant to what we do or might want to do."[125]

2. *Independence.* Autonomous individuals have their own opinion and behave according to it. "They accept or make rules for themselves. They are capable of forming their own independent judgements. Their thoughts and actions are not governed by other people, by tradition, by authority, or by psychological problems."[126]

3. *Self-control.* Autonomous individuals are not "swamped" by their own passions or needs. They are able to arrange and adjust their desires, ideals, and goals corresponding to "a hierarchical structure of some life plan."[127]

4. *Rational reflection.* Autonomous individuals contemplate and consciously think over what they do and who they believe. They subjugate

123. Hare, "Adolescents," 78.
124. McLaughlin, "Parental Rights," 78.
125. Dearden, "Autonomy," 450.
126. Thiessen, *Teaching*, 118.
127. Ibid.

their actions and convictions to reflection and criticisms. They are endowed with the sufficient and necessary knowledge to make intelligent decisions.

5. *Competence.* Autonomous individuals are able to implement the plans and projects they have made. They posses volition, determination, and every other "executive virtue" necessary for autonomous behavior.[128]

6. *Final note:* There is a consensus among educators that a person is not born autonomous. However, children have both the right and the natural tendency to develop their capacity for autonomy. If parents or educators don't create adequate space for the development of autonomy, it is an educational failure which often qualifies as neglect or indoctrination.[129]

Remember that the problem with autonomy is the absence of a measure of degree or extent. To what extent should individuals be free, independent, rational, and competent, to be identified as autonomous? The liberal theoreticians of education usually quietly assume an idealized concept of full autonomy, completely or perfectly (as in the previous cases, where they presupposed the ideal ability of the individual to recognize and work with evidence).[130]

In contrast, the teachers of character presuppose the concept of "normal autonomy," which recognizes that every component of autonomy (freedom, independence, rationality, and competence) is fundamentally limited. Children a) are not born independent, b) are always formed (conditioned) by a specific culture, c) never have an exhaustive amount of information for making completely autonomous decisions, d) never have the ideal rationality necessary for evaluating the information. In addition, says Thiessen, it seems that "human nature desires both dependency and autonomy, both community and individuality," "we want both to be loved, to belong, to be dependent on a group and to be autonomous, independent."[131] In other

---

128. Ibid., 119.

129. Haworth, *Autonomy*, 127.

130. Only rarely do we find authors who are willing to deal with this problem. They admit that absolute autonomy is unthinkable, and suggest terms like "autonomy to a relative extent," or "autonomy in an important respect," or "weak autonomy" (Dearden, "Autonomy," 458; Haydon, "Autonomy," 220). None of these formulations solve the problem, they only beg the question—exactly to what extent, in what respect, how "weak" should the desired autonomy be?

131. Thiessen, *Teaching*, 135, 141.

words—the freedom of an individual is never free from the freedom of the whole. The true meaning of the concept of socialization lies in the search for balance between the ideal of autonomy and the community, between dependence and independence.

Consequences or Effects of Indoctrination

Education is indoctrinational if it results in closed-mindedness on the part of the student, the liberally-oriented theoreticians of education agree.[132] Further—indoctrination occurs as the result of an educator's failure to cultivate a "critical openness."[133] If the desired result of education is "critical openness of the mind," what does that term mean? Thiessen, with reference to O'Leary, distinguishes several conditions which must be met in order to fulfill this ideal:

a. *Neutrality.* If a person with a closed mind is defined as one who "holds their beliefs as settled" and at the same time "committing,"[134] then critical openness, on the contrary, represents a neutral position towards any subject or doctrine. Gardner explains the concept by saying that being open-minded about alternatives means "not thinking these alternatives to be true or false."[135]

b. *Epistemic.* It has been said that indoctrinated individuals are those who hold their beliefs without regard to the evidence.[136] Critical openness, on the other hand, takes the evidence into account. Green and Snook distinguish four epistemic aspects of working with evidence. 1) Critically open individuals can give evidence for their beliefs. 2) They can take into account opposing evidence. 3) They are prepared to actively search out opposing evidence and weaknesses in their own system of beliefs. 4) Individuals with open minds are willing to revise and reassess their beliefs in light of new evidence and arguments.[137]

---

132. Cf. Hare, *Open-mindedness*, 8; Scruton et al., *Education*, 25.

133. Hare, *Open-mindedness*, 41.

134. O'Leary, "Indoctrinated," 295.

135. Gardner, "Religious," 92.

136. Green, "Beliefs."

137. Ibid., 33f; Snook, *Indoctrination*, 56.

c. *Truthfulness.* Critical openness is explicitly excluded from the concept of any kind of exclusivity, definitive or absolute truth.[138] It is just this claim to absolute truth which, according to the liberal thinkers, is a sign of narrow-mindedness or closed-mindedness.

d. *Methodological.* Critically open individuals methodically reflect on and doubt their beliefs. In this context, Hare cites Bertrand Russell, who said, "When you come to a point of view, maintain it with doubt. This doubt is precious because it suggests an open mind."[139] Critical openness is also associated with strict objectivity, impartiality, and tolerance towards the ideas of others.[140]

Criticism of the consequential criteria which teachers of character put forward is, in principle, the same as for all the preceding criteria. It is an idealized concept which doesn't take into account the limits of human nature or the limits of the educational situation as such. In other words, none of the above-mentioned conditions is actually feasible. Let's take the four given conditions, out of order. 1) There is no such thing as absolute neutrality. Everyone—including the therapeutically-oriented educators—holds onto some beliefs, i.e., they consider them to be "certain," "complete" or "closed," and they base their actions on them. Human thought necessarily springs from certain principles, premises, or assumptions which we consider to be "fundamental," that is, without need for any further evidence (for example, that cowardice is low, or that a triangle has three sides). 2) No one has complete epistemic certainty in all their beliefs. Not all the evidence is available to us, we cannot think through all the opposing evidence, and often don't even know how to evaluate the evidence. Nevertheless, we can make everyday moral judgments (e.g., stealing is bad). 3) No matter how much liberal thinkers don't allow the idea of any kind of absolute truth, that very claim of truthfulness is implicitly assumed in their arguments. If, in their opinion, indoctrinated individuals believe things which are "dubious" or "controversial," then individuals with open minds must be those who believe only what is *undoubtedly* and *undeniably* true. So are the liberal thinkers absolutely certain that no absolute truth exists? Is their claim that there is no truth, true? If yes, then once again we have run into self-referential inconsistency. 4) Is it possible to methodologically doubt everything about

---

138. Cf. Peshkin, *God's Choice*; Hare, *Open-mindedness.*

139. Ibid., 31.

140. Rokeach, *Open and Closed,* 4–5.

everything? Do the liberal therapeutists really doubt everything, or only everything except their liberal doctrines?

In opposition to the idealized concept of critical openness, the character educators again construct the concept of "normally critical openness." That—as the above-mentioned criticism indicates—envisions limitation(s), as much on the possibilities of human nature as on the nature of each educational situation. Criticality makes no sense by itself or for itself, but always supposes there is *something* to criticize. The "what" represents the rich cultural material the child acquires through education. There is no discussion about language, values, traditions, or habits, because the as-yet undeveloped potential of the child doesn't allow it. Children are born uncritical, dependent, conditioned, and if they are to acquire a healthy, that is, a normal degree, of criticality, they must first gain the fundamentals which are not subject to criticism. Each kind of education mediates this to its children. And that is the final argument regarding the criteria of consequences—the critical openness of the learner's mind is possible and desireable, but a) never to the idealized extent, i.e., absolutely, b) every education which strives for the cultivation of criticality—even the liberal-therapeutic one—necessarily has "uncritical" fundamental doctrines which are transmitted through education.

Conclusions about Indoctrination

What follows from this discussion? That every education is indoctrinational? As has already been said, it depends on how the concept is defined. According to the liberal-therapeutic definition, indoctrination is inevitable, but in my opinion that is not the best definition. Thiessen suggests another definition which has a better foundation both philosophically and pedagogically. It suggests that "the core idea of indoctrination be thought of as the curtailment of a person's growth towards normal rational autonomy."[141] Thiessen further fills out this brief definition with several basic comments.

a. The proposal to define indoctrination as a limitation on development is aimed more at people than at doctrines or doctrinal propositions. This redirection of attention onto people is given with the recognition that indoctrination shows manipulation not only of the mind or understanding, but manipulation of the whole person. Rationality

141. Thiessen, *Teaching*, 233.

is closely and inseparably linked to all the other elements of human personality—our past, social ties, emotions, physical state, etc. Indoctrination, then, is not only "brainwashing," as the therapeutists say, but also a "washing" of the emotions, relationships, habits, traditions, etc. Every totalitarian regime knows this very well.

b. Only when the principle of holistic integrity is firmly anchored, can we proceed to the question of limiting rational development, i.e., the cognitive capacity of humanity. Knowing that this is not the only area in which indoctrination can happen, it is good to consider some developmental-cognitive regularities. Any kind of cognitive development assumes that children in their early stages go through the processes of socialization, initiation, and the so-called acquisition of the primary culture, which are non-rational processes, as we saw above. To attach the pejorative term "indoctrination" to this stage for its non-rationality is a fundamental error. Children need to acquire their primary culture if they are to (not only cognitively) thrive. They also need that culture to be stable, safe, and coherent.

c. The developmental approach to the concept of indoctrination further recognizes that the meaning of the concept will change as the child matures. The development of a child begins with an initial phase that is necessarily non-rational, culturally specific, and in big quotes "coersive," meaning that children simply cannot choose which culture, language, values, etc. they will be devoted to. When children are born into a certain culture we don't speak of coercion, and therefore, when the children subsequently accept that culture we cannot speak of indoctrination. It is generally known that as children grow they ask questions, and this curiosity is supported by every normal parent and teacher. But what children in this stage need are answers, not doubts. It would be absurd and irresponsible to present them with a lecture on "methodical skepticism" at this stage. A pre-schooler is not a college student. When the initial phase is finished, children can gradually (an important word) come to know the reality that there also exist other traditions and cultures than their own—if they haven't already noticed it themselves. If teachers do not inform the children of this reality, or even conceal it from them, they are indoctrinating in the true sense of the word, says Thiessen.[142] Not until the next (adolescent) stage of

142. Ibid., 236.

cognitive development, which Piaget would probably call the stage of *formal operations*, can individuals be led to critical reflection of their own traditions, as well as alternative traditions—whether current or past. The gradualness and gentleness of the whole process is given on the one hand by the fact that individual stages are not strictly separated, and on the other hand that each individual develops individually. We have different predispositions—intelligently, emotionally, socially, and otherwise, so what might truly be indoctrination for one person is not necessarily indoctrination for another. In other words, educators lead each student in an individualized way from the state of complete dependency to a state of relative, or normal, independence when they no longer need a teacher because they have successfully internalized the moral principles. The meaning of the term indoctrination changes according to the stage or according to the individual on whom it is being done.

d. Real indoctrination thwarts the development of rationality, but when qualified as "normal," rationality is not idealized. Normal rationality involves and welcomes many traditional principles, such as concern for evidence, knowledge of different forms of knowing, cultivation of intellectual virtues like critical openness, etc., but at the same time, this concept is aware of the limits of human knowledge. It not only perceives the limited possibilities for objectivity in knowing, but also recognizes that empirical knowledge does not exhaust everything that can be known. Further, the concept of normal rationality understands that the justification of all specific doctrines or beliefs is always situated—socially, psychologically, culturally, historically, or otherwise. Reflective and open criticality in this context means that I am aware that the development of my criticality has taken place within the framework of a specific doctrinal community which has influenced my beliefs.

e. Indoctrination means a failure in the development of normal autonomy. Absolute autonomy is an empty ideal. It has already been said that normal autonomy strives for balance between the freedom of the individual and the freedom of the whole. It recognizes that no one is born autonomous, but is predisposed to autonomy. Normally autonomous individuals are aware of their dependence on their given community, that is, the need to belong, to share values, etc., while preserving a socially acceptable distance.[143] The concept of normal autonomy further allows that an individual can freely give it up—freely choose to submit themselves to an idea, a (loved) person, life mission, etc.

f. Indoctrination is not a phenomenon that concerns only educational institutions; moreover, it is the liberal theoreticians of education (Communist education, political education, religious education, etc.) who selectively choose what is to be considered indoctrination. It is necessary to take into account the wider social area that influences the development of children, youth and also adults—the media, advertising, goal-directed propaganda, and so on.

g. Indoctrination is a question of extent. In the liberal conception it was indicted as being a matter of "either/or." Specific people, institutions, and methods were swept under the table as a whole. But the developmental understanding of the phenomenon of indoctrination shows that it is always a question of degree. In one or another stage it is possible to indoctrinate to a certain extent or with a certain magnitude, depending on the cause, intent, or results of the indoctrination.

I conclude this chapter, which has in its title the question of whether it is possible to teach or learn goodness. We have seen a whole spectrum of answers. We have also seen two main streams that have significantly stood out during the second half of the twentieth century and which are still being applied today. Proponents of these streams differ in their answers not only in principle—*whether* it is possible to teach goodness, and if so, *how*. With a little simplification, it is possible to observe that the more the liberal (let's say, on the left side of the spectrum) is the anthropological starting point, the greater the unwillingness to implant any virtue, values, or goodness. Likewise, the more to the right, the more intensively we hear the appeal to teach, form, impart, and get accustomed to, virtues. Within their extreme positions is the traditional argument between liberal permissiveness and authoritarian totalitarianism. In the first case the educators follow the will of the individual, and in the second they are against it. But there is also a

---

143. Václav Bělohradský notes in relation to this problem that when a mainstream culture goes wrong—as, for example, under a totalitarian regime—every mature and responsible person has to deal with the question to what extent am I to participate on the culture so that I can be its contructive critic and not an enemy (see Bělohradský, *Společnost*).

third option, thoroughly desireable, but by far not as easily achieved as it may seem on the theoretical level. A unique demonstration of this kind of education was presented centuries ago by Jan Amos Comenuis. We will see that it overlaps in many ways the concepts of character education outlined above. Yet Comenius's work has its own inimitable character—language, eclecticity, synthesism, realism, etc.—which make his educational project unique. While it is true that many contemporary readers might find Comenius's philosophy and terminology archaic and difficult to understand, it isn't an insurmountable obstacle (with a little hermeneutical effort). Therefore I will devote the final chapter to Comenius's "methodus morum in specie," and will attempt to extract from it what is most helpful for the current practice of ethical education.

Chapter 8

Conclusion: Even When No One Is Looking
Comenius's "Method of Morals"

COMENIUS'S EMENDATIONAL (RESTORATIONAL) PROJECT, including his ethical education, is constructed on the basis of a wider philosophic-theological whole. As a theologian, he sees nature and the whole natural world as the creation, that is, the work of a Creator who created everything purposefully and meaningfully. As a philosopher (of education), he sees nature as a *"sub specie educationis,"*[1] that is, through the lens of education, so as to discover its educational potential. Thus, in the introductory part of his Great Didactic[2] he says that "everything that is, is for something."[3] The natural world is not an accidental occurance of things or the result of events that happen meaninglessly and come out of nowhere, but it is a

1. Compare Patočka, *Komeniologické*, 133.

2. In this chapter I will quote often from Comenius's *Didactica magna* [Great Didactic], which is Comenius's own edited Latin translation of his *Czech Didactic*. In this text I will rely on Keatinge's English translation of 1896; my own translations from the *Czech Didactic* will be indicated.

3. The complete text of the quotation in question is as follows: "By the voice of nature we understand the universal Providence of God or the influence of Divine Goodness which never ceases to work all in all things; that is to say, which continually develops each creature for the end to which it has been destined. For it is a sign of the divine wisdom to do nothing in vain, that is to say, without a definite end or without means proportionate to that end. Whatever exists, therefore, exists for some end, and has been provided with the organs and appliances necessary to attain to it. It has also been gifted with a certain inclination, that nothing may be borne towards its end unwillingly and reluctantly, but rather promptly and pleasantly, by natural instinct." Comenius, *Didaktika magna*, 40–41.

purposeful being, called to meaning. Everything that is, is "for," expounds Radim Palouš.[4] Everything is for some purpose, for something, towards something. Every thing, every being is characterized by its teleological nature. It has a goal that lies outside of itself, goes beyond itself; it exists this way, because for this it was intended and equipped. In Comenius's terminology, nothing exists "*samosvojně*" (i.e., by itself and for itself). In this divine contribution lies the educational potential of the natural world. By birth a person enters the school of the world, which, by its nature, educates the nature of the human being towards true humanity.

That a person needs such an education is obvious to Comenius. In the whole of creation, human beings are the only beings that are able to make themselves the ultimate goal of their existence, making themselves *homo mensura*, which, unlike antiquity or even modernity, is not considered something positive, but at the core of the human tragedy, which Comenius regards as the source of all human "confusions" and "bewilderments."[5] As people whose ultimate goal and end is within themselves, they are disturbingly out of order with the rest of creation, or with the universal harmony of all that is (as the "later" Comenius would say), because their attitude is unnatural, inauthentic, and improper. Not only does it tear people away from God, from whom flows all "life and breath itself," but it separates people from other people, as it "forces man to make himself the goal of his existence, that is, to love himself, to pay attention to himself, and care for himself first."[6]

How does Comenius explain this particularly human tendency? Right at the beginning of his *Czech Didactic* he rather widely interprets this paradoxical state and source of the human problem, which he intends to answer in his "didactic:"

> For what is in relation to people as it ought to be? What stands in its proper place? Nothing. Everything is upside down, everything has gone wrong, for all the order, all the government, all the noble features are scattered. Instead of the wisdom by which we were to resemble angels, there is foolishness and dullness . . . resembling dumb beasts. Instead of prudence, which leads one to prepare for eternity, for which we have been created, there is a forgetfulness

4. Palouš, *Komenského*.

5. Comenius often uses the terms *motaniny* and *jinudosti* (confusions and bewilderments) in his works to describe the human condition. For the earliest reference see *Hlubina bezpečnosti* [Center of Safety].

6. Kožmín and Kořmínová, *Zvětšeniny*, 60.

of both the eternal nature and the mortality of man. . . . Instead of mutual candidness and truthfulness, there is slyness, deceit, and falsity everywhere. Instead of grace, there is envy, instead of confidence, there is deception. . . . Instead of unity, there are discords, quarrels, and rages, secret malice as well as open hostility, fights and wars. Instead of righteousness, there are injustices, robberies, thefts; everyone greedily amasses only for himself or herself. Instead of purity, there is lechery, both internal and external; there is adultery, infidelity, misconduct, and lewdness, both in the mind and in speech. Instead of truthfulness, there are lies and gossip everywhere. Instead of humbleness, there is arrogance and pride, preening and boasting; one rising against the other. Woe to you, miserable generation, how deeply you have sunk into wretchedness![7]

Comenius came from a background with a traditional biblical narrative where human beings were presented as *imago Dei*, that is, as beings created for a fundamental relationship with God. Our characters are to reflect God's character, that is, a reflection of the *Summum Bonum*, the greatest possible conceivable good. However, as a result of the archetypical fall of humanity caused by our desire to be equal with God, we have lost our so-called *nexus hypostaticus*, which is the personal relationship of created beings with their Creator. In the desire to be gods, humankind closed themselves off, or "bent" into themselves, thereby alientating themselves from their natural, pre-ordained status that enabled such an important transcendence. The result of that distortion is the inability to fulfill their essential human calling, and the need for help and salvation. Thanks to the salvific act of Jesus Christ this salvation is not only possible, but—because of the miserable state of humanity—is also supremely desireable. All inhumanity needs to be done away with, guilt can and must be acknowledged and forgiven, which is the key spiritual principle through which comes the vitally important reconciliation of people with God, with others, and with themselves.

Education towards morality is an integral part of Comenius's emendational project. The importance he gave to moral, or ethical, education is clear from how often he made it his theme, explicitly emphasized it, and repeatedly returned to it in his various works. The problem of the morality of humanity as such, he most thoroughly dealt with in his *Světě mravním* [The Moral World], which forms the sixth degree of his *Pansofia*. He gave the

7. Comenius, *Didaktika česká*, 4–5.

most attention to ethical education in his *Didactics* (both *Great* and *Czech*), but also discussed it in other works.[8] In addition to little notes distributed in various other places in the *Didactics*, Comenius devoted a whole chapter to moral education (XXIII), called "The Method of Morals."[9]

In the very beginning of the chapter Comenius explains that everything which had come before was only "preparation" or "the beginning," and not the main work. Note that the preceding twenty-two chapters were about nothing less than his whole methodology for teaching "the sciences, art and language." But the main work, according to Comenius, was "the study of wisdom which elevates us and makes us steadfast and noble-minded . . . and draw nigh to God Himself," which is the work that fulfills the three fundamental pedagogical goals that the author announced at the beginning of the *Didactic*. Here Comenius clarifies that the teleological requirements of *knowledge, morality,* and *piety* flow from our *a priori* anthropological nature, meaning that to each person it is given 1) to be knowledgeable about things, 2) to have power over things and oneself, and 3) to turn to God, the source of everything.[10]

These three requirements are inseparable."[11] "For what is knowledge without morality?" Comenius asks rhetorically, and immediately answers with the old saying, "He who makes progress in knowledge but not in morality . . . , recedes rather than advances. And thus, what Solomon said of the beautiful but foolish woman, holds good of the learned man who possesses not virtue: 'As a jewel of gold in a swine's snout, so is a fair woman which is without discretion.'"[12] Therefore, an education that was not held together by the "unbreakable bonds" of morality and piety, would be an "unhappy" education. "In order that humanity not fall into inhumanity,"[13] people need the kind of education that will develop humanity in all three

8. See, for example, *Informatorium školy mateřské, Pampaedia, Pravidla chování.*

9. Most of the quotations I will use in this section come from that 23rd chapter of the *Great Didactic*, therefore I will reference only those coming from other chapters or sources.

10. See Comenius, *Great Didactic,* 46, where he presents his pedagogical theology. See also his *Světě mravním,* where he develops this basic anthropological triad in other contexts as well, e.g., philosophical, scholarly, irenical, and so on.

11. Comenius clarifies the theme of the indivisibility of the individual educational areas in chapter 10, dealing with "universal" education. See *Didactica magna,* 70–75.

12. Ibid.

13. Comenius repeated this idea many times in various places. See, for example, *Pampaedia,* II:8.

dimensions. For "the whole excellence [*essence* in the *Czech didactic*] of man," Comenius explains (in chapter IV), is situated in these three things, "for they alone are the foundations of the present and of the future life. All other things (health, strength, beauty, riches, honor, friendship, good-fortune, long life) are as nothing, if God grant them to any, but extrinsic ornaments of life, and if a man greedily gape after them, engross himself in their pursuit, occupy and overwhelm himself with them to the neglect of those more important matters, then they become superfluous vanities and harmful obstructions."

Comenius consistently maintains the close connection between knowledge and morality in similar ways, in his other didactic works. For example, the *Orbis pictus* (*The World in Pictures*) is a small encyclopedia of the world in which, with the help of pictures, the reader can not only come to know how the world *is*, but also how it *should be*, or *shouldn't* be. It is possible to identify this approach in almost every picture in the book. For illustration I present a picture which, in addition to showing the simple "fact" of fire, which a student can learn to recognize in various languages, also shows the value of its *use* and *misuse* (a fire where it belongs, in the fireplace, and a conflagration outside the window).[14]

14. Taken from *Orbis pictus*, pict. 7.

It is worth noting the didactic strategy by which the author communicates moral content, without using any explicit moral argument. Just by choosing this stylistic means, the author enables the reader to learn moral contexts (positive and negative), uses and abuses, along with the facts, without any moralizing.[15]

The "core" or cardinal virtues are the actual subjects of moral education in Comenius's *Didactics*. They are the four well-known—from antiquity—virtues *prudence, temperance, fortitude,* and *justice,* without which, according to Comenius, the structure of pedagogy would be "without a foundation." Comenius first briefly clarifies and explains the individual virtues, and then presents the method of their acquisition, which forms the core of his "method of morality." There are six principles given in the *Czech Didactic,* which are enlarged and extended to ten in the later *Great Didactic.*[16] For the sake of clarity and economy I will only summarize them here:

1. Virtue is cultivated by actions, not by talk. For man is given life "to spend it in communication with people and in action." Without virtuous actions man isn't anything more than a meaningless burden on the earth.

2. Virtue is in part gained by interactions with virtuous people. An example is the education Alexander received from Aristotle.

3. Virtuous conduct is cultivated by active perseverence. A properly gentle and constant occupation of the spirit and body turns into diligence, so that idleness becomes unbearable for such a man.

4. At the heart of every virtue is service to others. Inherent in fallen human nature is enormous self-love, which has the effect that "everyone wants most of the attention." Thus it is necessary to carefully instill the understanding that "we are not born only for ourselves, but for God and our neighbor."

5. Cultivation of the virtues must begin at the earliest age, before "ill manners and vice begin to nest." In the same way that it's easy to mold wax and gypsum when they're soft, but once they've hardened it's impossible to re-shape them, so also with men: most of one's character is based on the first "skills" that are instilled in early childhood.

---

15. Cf. Menck, "Formation," 261–75.

16. The question is whether they are truly clearer in the extended version. The attentive reader can't avoid noticing that some of the principles overlap in the "great" version.

6. Honor is learned by virtuous action. As he learns to "walk by walking, to speak by speaking, to read by reading" etc., so a person learns "to obey by obedience, forbearance by delays, veracity by speaking truth" and so on.

7. Virtue is learned by example. "For children are like monkeys: everything they see, whether good or bad, they immediately want to imitate, even when they're told not to, and thus they learn to imitate before they learn how to learn." Therefore they need "living examples" as instructors.

8. Virtue is also learned by instruction, which has to accompany example. Instructing means clarifying the meaning of the given rule of moral behavior, so as to understand why they should do it, what they should do, and why they should do it that way. Similarly, as "by a thorn a beast is pushed to move or to run, so a successful mind is not only told but also urged by gentle words to run to virtue."

9. It's necessary to protect children from bad people and influences. Insasmuch as a child's mind is easily infected, it is necessary on the one hand to retreat from "evil society" and on the other hand to avoid lazy people. For the man who is idle "learns to do evil, because a mind cannot be empty; if it isn't carrying something useful, it fills itself with empty, useless and vile things."

10. Virtue requires discipline. Inasmuch as fallen human nature reveals itself to be constantly "here and there," it's necessary to systematically discipline it.

Comenius considered the final principle of the method, discipline, to be such an important element in the formation of character that he devoted a special chapter to it: chapter XXVI.[17] Here is where he first states his famous simile, "a school without discipline is like a mill without water." It does not follow from this, however, that our schools should "resound with shrieks and with blows. What we demand is vigilance and attention on the part of the master and of the pupils." Comenius expresses his fundamental resistance to force in his motto: *Omnia sponte fluant, absit violentia rebus,*

---

17. Again, for better readability I will not individually reference each citation, since in the following paragraphs dealing with discipline the vast majority come from chapter XXVI of the *Great Didactic*. References from the *Czech Didactic* and the *Analytical Didactic* will be noted.

or "let everything flow spontaneously, without violence."[18] This principle is more explicitly stated in the *Analytical Didactic*: "We wish that beating and anger be far away from something as sacred as the education of the spirit."[19] The educated spirit is a disciplined spirit, and if educators are to help students reach this desired goal it is necessary that they themselves well understand (a) the purpose, (b) the material, and (c) the method of discipline, that is, they know why, when, and how to discipline.

a. Comenius understands the purpose of discipline as the *goal of education*. An educator must be clear about why to discipline, for what purpose, and which goal. That children behave in all kinds of undisciplined ways, and therefore "against those who err it is necessary to use discipline," is without debate for Comenius. However, discipline should not be used "because they err," Comenius emphasized, "but in order that they may not err again in the future." Discipline for this purpose is used "without anger or dislike, and should be exercised with such frankness and sincerity of purpose, that even the pupils may feel that the action taken is for their good, and that those set over them are but exercising paternal authority . . . and will thus regard it in the same light as a bitter draught prescribed for them by the doctor." The purpose of discipline, then, according to Comenius, is primarily preventative in nature, and its effectiveness is conditioned by mutual understanding. Both teachers and students must understand why the discipline is being given.

It is worth noting Comenius's psychological insight, that awareness of the ultimate goal of discipline restrains the educator's temperament. The impulsiveness, anger, or outburst of rage which is usually called forth in a disciplinary situation can be better managed by the teacher or parent if it is clear where it is headed. Anger, miscarriage of justice, humiliation, or decimation of the child manifests the failure of the educator and leads nowhere. The goal of discipline is to help children be better—to become better human beings. In that moment it is not about the teacher, nor in a certain sense is it about the student, either. Comenius knows neither teacher-centrism nor child-centrism. This is about the educational thing itself, that is, about humanity.

18. Comenius put this motto on the title page of his crowning didactic work, the *Opera didactica omnia*.

19. Comenius, *Didaktika analytická*, 42.

Awareness of such a goal significantly influences both the means of its application and the educator as well. The ultimate purpose of Comenius's education, and therefore of discipline, is the formation of authentic humanity. Recall Comenius's statement that "if a man is to become a man, he must be educated."[20] Discipline towards humanity must always be humane, and a good teacher knows it.

b. The second aspect of discipline is the "material" or subject of the discipline, and that can be twofold. a) If a student has no interest in studying, Comenius urges restraint in punishment. The lack of interest in study is not the problem of the student but that of the teacher. "For if studies are properly organized, they form in themselves a sufficient attraction, and entice all (with the exception of monstrosities) by their inherent pleasantness. If this be not the case, the fault lies not with the pupil, but with the master, and if our skill is unable to make an impression on the understanding, our blows will have no effect. Indeed, by any application of force we are far more likely to produce a distaste for letters than a love for them." b) However, in the case of moral misconduct, Comenius advises a more vigorous approach. As examples of such wrongdoing he offers obscenity, defiance, stubborn malice, pride, arrogance, or any evidence of impiety. Why is it necessary to proceed vigorously towards these offenses? Because moral misconduct is "an insult to God's majesty . . . and undermines the foundation of all virtue." Comenius knows that without virtue or moral standards, not only the schools but all of human society is as a mill without water. It doesn't work. Therefore, he recommends "expiating"[21] these offenses "with extremely severe punishment." What is meant by extremely severe punishment? Comenius's answer is explained in the next paragraph, which deals with the third aspect of discipline, its method.

c. The method of discipline. Comenius distinguishes three or four methods of discipline, which essentially express what we call progressive sanctions today. He derives the principle from the operations of

20. Comenius, *Didactica magna*, 67. It is similar to the equally famous statement by Immanuel Kant, which is set in a different—somewhat deterministic—context of thought: "A man can become a man only by education. He is nothing more than what education makes him." See Kant, *O výchově*, 34.

21. This is how Keatinge translated the Latin term *piandum*. In the *Czech Didactic* (his original language), Comenius used the word *usmířit*, which means "appease" or "reconcile." Keatinge's translation thus seems to be somewhat unfortunate in this case.

nature, namely he helps himself by using the illustration of the sun, "which, as it rises, gives a) light and heat always, b) sometimes rain and wind, c) rarely thunder and lightning."[22] Similarly, educators will best support the youth in their tasks if they a) always show, by continuous and living example, what is appropriate, b) with instructive words, reminders and sometimes even reprimands, make sure no one is corrupted, and only finally c) use the sharpest means, bodily. Comenius uses the Latin term *violentia remedia* (carried out with force) for these extreme means.[23] But at the same time he reminds us that it is necessary "to be careful not to use these extreme means for just any reason, or for very slight ones, lest they get worn down before the extreme case happens." Comenius emphasizes again that when educators have to use the extreme solution, "let them remove every bitter tone from their words, angry expression from their face and every cruelty from each blow, so that the students themselves are convinced that [the teachers] are not indulging in wrathful malice, but have the good of the students in mind."[24]

As the ultimate level of discipline for those who have "such an unfortunate nature that every milder means is inadequate," Comenius permits expulsion of that individual from school to prevent the others from being corrupted or obstructed. However, excluding a child from the educational process is the worst sorrow for Comenius, because for him education has a soteriological (salvational) meaning. Education is part of the *emendatio rerum humanarum*, i.e., the restoration of human affairs. Everyone needs an education that would restrain their human tendency to sin. People with the least restraint are exactly those who need education the most. They need *e-ducatio* in the proper meaning of the word, that is, to be trained up to be more noble, better, more humane.[25] That is why Comenius strongly urges

---

22. It must be added that Comenius's pedagogical principles, founded in his natural philosophy, are strictly conditioned by the climactic zone in which Comenius lived. But I am sure he would find some helpful principle in nature even if he had lived in central Africa.

23. In Comenius, *Czech Didactic*, 183, he describes this level in the following words: "To whomever then is stubborn, and for whom a milder word of discipline is not enough, can and should come true punishment."

24. Comenius, *Analytical Didactic*, 42.

25. Cf. Palouš's term *e-ducation* in his *Čas výchovy*, 63.

teachers to "try everything, before leaving anyone as ground totally unfit for education and considering them as lost."

In conclusion, Comenius emphasizes that every method of discipline must be used in such a way that students "may love and reverence their masters, and not merely allow themselves to be led in the right direction, but actually tend towards it of their own accord." And the summarization of it all is that "the object of discipline should be to stir us up to revere God, to assist our neighbors, and to perform the labors and duties of life with alacrity."

Comenius, Timely and Timeless

Is there a way in which Comenius's conception could enrich today's discussion about ethical education? It depends on who it is and from which research point of view they approach the subject, and also, with which ideological pre-understanding. Psychologists look at Comenius's contribution differently than didacticians, who see it differently than theologians, and different still than sociologists and philosophers of education. I will attempt to synthesize a summary of the positive insights of researchers and will add a few of my own.

Psychology

Although psychology did not exist as a science in Comenius's time, he anticipated many principles which were highly regarded even by thinkers who otherwise criticized him. For example, Jean Piaget noted that "if we go into the details of [Comenius's] theory of education, founded on spontaneous development, we are surprised by how modern the series of statements is, even with the absence of a clearly defined theory of the relationship between action and thought."[26] Comenius did not cover this area exhaustively in his method, nevertheless with "admirable intuition," according to Piaget, he formulated a series of principles refining the educational process from a psychological perspective; for example, the dependency of cognitive function and action, the principle of positive and affective motivation, the principle of consecutive development, principles that facilitate and inhibit the educational process, the principle of cooperation in the teacher-student

26. Piaget, *Comenius.*

relationship, and so on.[27] Piaget even saw in Comenius "the forerunner of the idea of developmental psychology and the founder of a system of progressive instruction adapted to the student's level of development."[28] Václav Kulič spoke in the same spirit, appreciating in Comenius's didactics "much [of what is] stimulating, what anticipates and confirms some of the current trends and approaches in the area of the psychology of human learning and its management.[29]" Cipro similarly evaluates the unique elements of the learning process in Comenius as "the integration of logic and psychology."[30] Ladislav Kratochvíl describes Comenius's psycho-didactic principles as an example "of timeless pedagogical realism."[31] Likewise, Jan Patočka appreciates that long before the possibility of experimental verification of his principles, Comenius, in his moral education, looked into and identified such laws as learning through action, the influence of the peer group, the principle of active participation, the principle of systematics, the principle of appropriateness, the principle of imitation, the importance of moral examples, the need for preventative measures, etc.[32] In spite of his archaic language, Comenius again and again amazes with his almost "prophetic vision," says Piaget in another quote.[33]

However, I believe all of that was not Comenius's main contribution. His ability to recognize these psychological principles is certainly deserving of wonder, because he did it without the tools of modern empirical science. Contemporary pedagogy knows them well today. The methodological issues of character formation have been scrutinized and treated from many perspectives and to an extent that Comenius could never have reached.[34]

27. See also Srogoň, "Basic Principles," 107–11; Marklund, *School Stages*, 55–63; Čapková, "Impact," 11–28.

28. Piaget, *Comenius*.

29. Kulič, "Comenius," 177.

30. Cipro, *Prameny*, 410.

31. Kratochvil, "Realismus," 123.

32. Patočka, *Komeniologické*, 48.

33. Piaget, *Comenius*.

34. Although many modern psychologists are complimenting Comenius from the psychological perspective, the fact remains that Comenius was not a psychologist in the modern sense of the word. Only the "invention" of experimentation has enabled us to uncover, develop, and verify the vast amount of pedagogical-psychological data that has incorporated pedagogy into the sciences (albeit the humanities, the "soft" sciences). For a hint of this massive research see, e.g., Loevinger, *Ego*; Čapek, *Odměny*; Langová and Vacínová, *Jak se*; Vágnerová, *Psychologie*; Vacek, *Rozvoj*.

Yet I believe that the truly stimulating effect of his "method of morality" lies elsewhere. See the following paragraphs.

Realistic Anthropology

As I suggested previously in the fourth chapter, the question of whether people are good or bad has four basic answers. If we distinguish the ontological from the moral nature of human beings, these four variants follow logically:

a. *anthropological pessimism*—we are not good ontologically or morally,

b. *anthropological romanticism*—we are good both ontologically and morally,

c. *anthropological realism*—we are good ontologically but morally lacking,

d. *existentialism*—we are ontologically bad but morally good.

It is an outline, a simplification, but it still allows a certain reflection of our ethical-educational process. Let's start with the last variant. Existential philosophers—especially the atheistic ones—are convinced that in themselves (ontologically), people are insignificant; they are simply "cast" into a burdened, meaningless existence and the freedom associated with it.[35] If the lives of individuals take on any meaning, it is only that meaning they decide to give themselves. Petříček interprets Sartre as saying, "At first, [man] is nothing: he will only be. And he will be what he will do."[36] Existence preceeds essence. No matter what they decide, there does not exist any *a priori* nature of human beings, nor any transcendental arbitor of truth that could judge what is good and what is bad. The first and most basic thing is to decide. Sartre speaks of "complete" or "absolute" freedom as the way of existence of a person who, in his judgment, is a "self-defining and self-determining insignificance."[37] Echoes of such a view of anthropology can be noticed in the ethical-educational literature from the second half of the twentieth century.

---

35. Existentialism is traditionally divided into theistic and atheistic: Sartre himself divided them the same way and subscribed to the latter; see Sartre, *Existentialism*. The theistic existentialists naturally see the human situation differently. Cf. Petříček, *Úvod*.

36. Petříček, *Úvod*, 102–3.

37. Allen, "Rational Autonomy," 201.

The first three variants are much more frequent. Comenius stands in the tradition of anthropological realism. In order to evaluate this concept, let us first consider the competing positions once more. Educators who believe that people are completely, perfectly, fully good—both ontologically and morally—see no need to shape individuals towards some good, but only to permissively observe or look after them, and assist them in their own self-development (see the romantic therapeutists). Educators from the opposite end of the spectrum, who consider people to be all bad—again, both ontologically and morally—are inclined to authoritarianism, or totalitarian control, transformation, taming, supervision, and the like (see the totalitarian pedagogical systems). Marginal note: a society or whole culture which adopts a romantic model tends towards sentimentality. A culture that presupposes the pessimistic model of human beings, tends towards cynicism. It seems to me that current Western culture is a mixture of both trends—we are deformed by diverse unscrupulous totalities (such as the dictator of profit, success, growth, etc.), but we survive it thanks to "regular doses of emotion."

In his anthropology, Comenius is neither a romantic-optimist nor a skeptic-pessimist.[38] He recognizes the tremendous potential of humans as beings who are "the most perfect and most valuable" of all creation, but who also know that the "sons of men" are a race that is "perverse," "half-hearted," "fickle," "blind," and that everything human is "out of joint."[39] Anthropological realism means the ability to acknowledge the contradictions of human nature. Comenius knows that humans can fall into inhumanity. In their being humans have immeasurable dignity and worth—because they were given to be the *imago Dei*. In their actions, however, they are problematic, capable of evil—as has been said, not always nor in everything, but too often they don't do what they should, or they do what they should not. Thus, we observe that every human capacity, every piece of knowledge, every skill, every competence (even school-based ones) can have either a positive or negative outworking. They can be used for good, but also for evil. Hence, the need for pedagogical formation of character— we are depraved and cannot become virtuous by ourselves, on the contrary, we have a tendency to "fill ourselves with empty, useless, and vile things,"

38. Anthropological optimism/pessimism is not to be confused with pedagogical optimism/pessimism. Comenius was a pedagogical optimistic precisely because he was an anthropological realist, that is, he believed that people are neither totally corrupt nor totally alright.

39. Cf. the introductory chapters of Comenius, *Didactica magna*.

says Comenius.[40] If human beings are to become what they should be, they must be led to it, educated, humanized. And exactly this is one of the greatest assets of Comenius's anthropology. If the romantic concept implies "sentimentalization" of human being, and the pessimistic concept implies "cynicization," then realism implies humanization, humane-ness, realization of the potential they have been given, the fulfilling of their human calling. People, you are someone (ontologically), so learn to act accordingly (morally).

The quality of Comenius's anthropology is well-illustrated in practical applications. Consider, for example, the current debate on the use of corporal punishment in education. The debate goes along the lines of either/or logic. Both camps are clear in what they believe, one says "beat them," the other says "forbid it legislatively." In many European countries, it is already the case that using corporal punishment threatens removal of a child from its family. Comenius's approach is again different, more subtle. His fine, that is, complex, distinction of the complexities of human nature allow him to go deeper. His anthropology, recognizing the ontological grandeur of human beings, prevents the authoritarian treatment of an individual as an inferior. Children are not "material" for educational machining. All educational activities are determined by the dignity of the human calling. From that comes Comenius's rejection of force. On the other hand, awareness of the characteristic human tendency towards immorality, which the educator can expect (and not only from the children), functions as a preventative to the child-centered idealization of children as *by nature* unsullied, obedient, hardworking, and desirous of knowledge. Children know how to be evil, brutal, and cruel, often being more cruel than adults. They are easy to influence, they can even get to a pathological—Comenius calls it "sinful"— extreme. In such a case Comenius proposes a *violentia remedia*. Whether nobility prevails over depravity, humanity over inhumanity, depends on many factors, and education is one of the most important. This is why for Comenius education is so precious and discipline so important—it is an expression of respect for the fundamental purpose of humanity as such. To not discipline children (or adults) who are lazy, disobedient, felonious, or malicious, would mean harming them, cultivating inhumanity in them, neglecting the dignity to which they are called.

Either/or logic is oversimplified because it presupposes that people are either good or bad—if they are good, don't discipline, if they are bad

---

40. Comenius, *Didaktika česká*, 158.

then beat, beat, beat. Comenius says—I am paraphrasing—it depends on how good or how corrupt one or another individual is. What did they do? For what reason? If I punish them, what do I want to accomplish? What is the ultimate goal of all educational activities? What means are adequate for such a goal? It seems that Jaroslava Pešková was very right to say that Comenius was not "great for his answers to the questions of his time, but for his questions, which expressed the key problems of the day."[41]

Wholeness, Nature, Harmony

This triad plays a fundamental role in Comenius's educational system. He tirelessly repeats the three concepts *omnes, omnia, omneno*, which express "the perspective of the whole."[42] Specifically, it means that it is necessary 1) to educate "everyone" (*omnes*), because all people—men and women, rich and poor, quick and slow—are created in the image of God and thus have the potential to display that image with dignity. 2) In order to fulfill this potential they have to be educated in "everything" (*omnia*) that is needed, which concretely means—to be knowledgeable, to have power over things, to use things appropriately, that is, piously. Which—in current terminology—corresponds to the so-called cognitive, volitional, and spiritual components of education. 3) The concept *omneno* expresses that all education is to be done "by every possible means" provided by nature, both that of the natural world and human nature. A pre-arranged harmony prevails between the two kinds of nature, the world is the macrocosm and each person is a microcosm. If educators will listen carefully to nature, they will discover what is needed for educating human nature, by way of "syncrizes" (Comenius's term),[43] because all natural reality is endowed with educational potential.

It is worth pointing out the close connection between knowledge, morality, and piety implied by Comenius's system. Remember Comenius's rhetoric question: What is education without morality? Or morality without the piety? In this emphasis is where Comenius most differs from the concepts of Enlightenment (and post-Enlightenment) modernity. She (modernity), overwhelmed by success in the field of science, began to believe in automatic advancement in the field of morality. The more people know,

41. Pešková, "Aktuální aspekty," 5.
42. Cf. Pelcová, "Druhy," 1.
43. On the term of syncrizes see Hábl, *Ultimate Human Goals.*

the more human they will be—in the sense of humaneness. After all, the one who "rightly" knows will "rightly" act. Comenius doesn't believe that education by itself will lead to morality (or piety). It is just the opposite.[44] It is precisely because knowledge cannot guarantee morality that it is necessary to accompany it with moral education. When this does not happen, it is contrary to human nature, an "unhallowed separation," because to people it is given not only to be knowledgeable about things, but also to use that knowledge well (which also glorifies the Creator).[45] Without it, people are not truly educated; they can be taught, but without morality they are "unnecessary burdens on the earth," even a "misfortune" to themselves and to others, for the more knowledge, the worse it is when misused for evil. That is why Comenius thinks that a humanity which is knowledgeable but immoral goes backwards, instead of forewards, it degenerates. In contrast, his "school as a forging-place of humanity,"[46] consciously strives for regeneration, that is, the re-birth of every dimension of humanity—intellectual, character, and spiritual (i.e., morals, knowledge and piety).[47]

Ne/samosvojnost[48]

We have seen that all of Comenius's educational works are permeated with the motif of *nesamosvojnost*. He first explicitly discusses this principle in

---

44. Here I argue with Menck's interpretation in his treatise on the formation of conscience, where he suggests that Comenius believed in a moral "automatism by which conscience follows knowledge—provided the knowledge was true." Menck derives this conclusion from his interpretation of Comenius's illustrations in the *Orbis pictus*. But I think this is a rash conclusion that does not take into account the other didactic works of Comenius. If Comenius believed that morality came automatically with knowledge, it would be logical for his *Didactics* to focus only on the cognitive level of education. But in fact, he speaks against Menck's supposition by insisting on the education of morals and contriving the most important methodological principles, in addition to educating the intellect. For more information, see Menck, "Formation," 261–75.

45. Comenius, *Didactica magna*, 74.

46. Comenius, *Obecná porada*, 367.

47. Palouš notes that Comenius was a scientist, but not of science in the sense of "a science of the world, how it lies and stands, but of the world as a common event, the world in a good and bad state; human knowing must understand this state: if something is out of order, it is essential for the components of true science to fix it." See Palouš, *Komenského*, 65.

48. I am not translating the term, for there is no one English word that would capture the proper meaning. The term will be expanded upon in the following paragraphs.

his early work, *Hlubina bezpečnosti* (*The Depths of Safety*, or *Centrum securitatis*), which came from his pre-didactic period. But it also appears in *The Labyrinth, Didactics* and later works like *Unum necessarium* (*The One Necessary Thing*). It is a somewhat older term, but has a rich content. Its anthropological foundation is Comenius's experience that "everyone, always and everywhere needs some sure and firm foundation of safety for body and soul."[49] Inspired by Mikuláš Kusánský, Comenius developed the metaphor of the world as a wheel: if it is to roll well, it must be well-anchored in the center. The perfect center of a wheel is—as opposed to the spokes and frame—unmoving, stable, safe. It is an attribute of God which only the Creator of the "wheel" has. According to Comenius, every problem of human beings and their world are the result of the breaking away of the "wheel" from its center. In order to grasp the precariousness of the human situation, Comenius proposes this term, *samosvojnost*. He defines it as the state in which a person "has twisted God's order of things," and "wants in and of themselves to be the source of their own existence, their own counselor, guide, guardian, lord, idol."[50] *Samosvojnost* thus alienates humans not only from their Creator, but also from one another, because it causes "man to make himself his own goal, to love, desire and care for only himself."[51] People forget that "their life and even breath itself flow to them from God," and ascribe everything either to their own merits or to blind luck. This is, according to Comenius, the universal human situation: "There is not even one person who could keep God and his will wholly in their hearts, able to resist *svojnost* and bewilderment: we have all been plunged into this, one more in one way, the other more in another way, we all put ourselves above decency, we all care excessively for ourselves, listen more to ourselves than necessary, delight too much in ourselves."[52] The consequence of this state is all the human "wandering" in the labyrinth of this world.

The connection with moral education is obvious. We saw that Comenius's "method of morality" is in principle the didactic answer to the problem of *samosvojnost*. In the fourth principle Comenius explicitly says that human nature has been "broken by the wretched error of self-love," which is expressed in that "everyone wants care to be devoted only to themselves ... everyone cares only for their own things" and cares nothing at all about

49. Comenius, *Hlubina*, 18.
50. Ibid., 36.
51. Kožmín and Kožmínová, *Zvětšeniny*, 60.
52. Comenius, *Hlubina*, 49–50.

others or "the happy state of public things." Against this human "poverty" there is only one medicine," says Comenius in *The Depths of Safety*, "a return to the center, which is God."[53] This essential movement towards the center is very close to the "return to the Paradise of the Heart" in the later *Labyrinth*. In *The Depths of Safety* Comenius called it *resignare* (resignation). But he doesn't mean that in the modern sense of the word—as something negative, hopeless and undesireable, but just the opposite: not resignation *to*, but resignation *from*. People see their futile efforts, stop seeking and groping around in places where there is nothing, and with hope return to the place which gives their lives meaning, peace and safety in the midst of all troubles. It is a "resignation from worldiness as it appears in the current time," says Palouš.[54] In other words, it is a resignation from dependency on anything changeable or temporary.

Comenius writes in the same spirit in the *Great Didactic*. The youth are to be carefully instilled with the understanding that "we are born not for ourselves alone, but for God and our neighbor ... and that they be seriously persuaded of this truth and will learn from their boyhood to imitate God" and the whole creation, which has been prepared to benefit not only itself but the whole.[55]

For Comenius, therefore, *samosvojnost* is unequivocally undesirable and immoral. We humans were not created for ourselves and don't belong to ourselves. Comenius's concept implies a deep and paradoxical anthropological principle—the more preoccupied with themselves individuals are, the less human they are; the more they want to find themselves, the more they lose themselves, and vice versa, those who manage to forget or lose themselves, find true humanity. This is the order of creation. The task of moral education is to usher students into this order, to make them right-minded people by giving them that which will help them overcome their crooked tendency towards *samosvojnost*. The process will always be challenging, it will require a lot of work both on the part of the teacher and of the student. It is no less than an essential turn, *metanoia*, change of view, repentance. Humble individuals admit their *samosvojnost* as a problem and consciously set themselves on the path of humanity. In current terminology, any progress in the area of moral competence begins with the recognition and admission of incompetence. Growth in (not only moral) competence

53. Ibid., 51.
54. Palouš, *Komenského*, 10.
55. Comenius, *Didaktika magna*, 214.

presupposes the discovery that I am not as competent as I should be.[56] The fact is that the process of accepting this reality is neither easy nor pleasant. Perhaps that is why the concept of *repentance* has disappeared from modern educational methods. But Comenius recognizes it, and even considers this innermost turn as the key to moral cultivation of humanity. Recall the turning of Comenius's pilgrim in the moment of transition from *the Labyrinth of the World* into the *Paradise of the Heart*, or the *nexus hypostaticus* in the *Great Didactic*. Only that touching of the sacred, the absolute good (*summum bonum*), awakens the desire for the true good, and at the same time, the desire to overcome the evil we see within us.

A marginal note: in today's school systems, the concept of competitive ability is very common. It is called "education to competitive ability."[57] It's not a bad thing, but if it should be the ultimate goal of the educational process, I would be worried about the future. Speaking affectively, when I'm old I would like to have around me at least one *non-samosvojnost* individual for every hundred competitively-able ones.

Spirituality: The *Nexus Hypostaticus*

The next and final motif in Comenius's ethical education, unsurprisingly ubiquitous, is spirituality. It is closely connected with the previous motif of *non-samosvojnost*. People have a spiritual nature in the sense that their physicality does not exhaust their whole essence. We have seen that Comenius expresses human spirituality with the term *nexus hypostaticus*. It refers to the personal connection between the created being and the Creator. Comenius introduces the term in the first chapter of the *Great Didactic*, where he clarifies why people are the "most excellent" of all creatures. He paraphrases the biblical message (Psalm 8) to humankind, "I have given Myself in personal communion (*nexus hypostaticus*), joining My nature to thine for eternity . . ., know therefore that thou art the corner-stone and epitome . . . the representative of God . . . and crown of My glory."[58] The spirituality of these realities is also given by the fact that we don't have them engraved "on the temple doors." Or in the "titles of books," nor do we have

---

56. Cf. Plesu, *Minima*.

57. This is a massive operational program to support European education. For details see http://www.op-vk.cz/ (accessed October 31, 2015).

58. Comenius, *Didaktika magna*, 25–26.

them "in our eyes or ears," but "in our hearts," that is, in our very nature.[59] The dignity and value of human beings is also expressed in the fact that when creation fell into evil, the Creator didn't come to hate them, but gave Himself to them, even sacrificing Himself to save them. That is the essence of the gospel didactic, which communicates the fundamental message regarding human identity: men and women, you are worth saving. Comenius was heard on more than one occasion to say that he considered his educational calling as a spiritual effort, namely, as part of a soteriological plan in which he is to work on the remedy of human affairs.[60]

This aspect of Comenius's work was a thorn in the side of those who interpreted his legacy through the prism of materialism, atheism, or Communism. Comenius's spirituality, as well as all of his metaphysics, was considered the "residual of the time."[61] Some of the more radical ones even spoke of it as "medieval mud that was glued to Comenius' feet" or a "speculative wasteland" without much meaning.[62] What was of value from Comenius was merely his "didactology." But for Comenius's education, spirituality was foundational, so any interpretation that wants to fulfill its task with integrity must take that into account. This is why I am raising the interpretive question: What is the potential for ethical education, of the spiritual motif of a "personal connection" between the Creator and creation?

---

59. Ibid., 26.

60. See Comenius's statement "*Ego quae pro iuventute scripsi, non ut paedagogus scripsi, sed ut theologus*" (whatever I have written for youth, I haven't written as a teacher, but as a theologian) in his *Opera didactica omnia*, 27. He speaks similarly in Comenius, *Methodus*, see especially the chapter called "Oslovení teologů." (*VSJAK 6, Work 15 / II*, 91–361. Czech translation of J. Šmaha issued 1892.)

61. Popelová, *Komenského*, 143.

62. Other Comeniologists from the Communist (or socialist) period of modernity also interpret Comenius in a similar spirit. František Tichý, for example, writes in his introduction to Comenius's didactic works, "The religious form contrasts with the revolutionary content of Comenius' views on schooling and education. Outwardly . . . Comenius remains in the Middle Ages, but in the internal content he shows the way forward, away from theology and feudalism, through capitalism to socialism. Comenius, as a typical representative of his time, trudges along with his feet still in the mud and confusion of medieval times, but looking daringly across several centuries ahead, shows in large part the way for us, too, as builders of a classless society, builders of socialism and Communism. How absurd and pointless it is, therefore, when some people look for the meaning and explanation of Comenius' pedagogical legacy in the medieval mud clinging to his feet." See Tichý, "S Komenským," 9–10. Compare also Alt, *Pokrokovy*; Krasnovskij, *Komenský*.

First—humans, as created beings, begin by admitting that the concept of good is a puzzle. A secret, a mystery. *Finitum non capax infinitum.*[63] It is not within human strength to define it. Perhaps evil—is the lack of good.[64] But what is good? G. E. Moore was right when he said that the concept of "good" is one of those concepts that are "incapable of definition . . ., because they are the ultimate terms of reference to which whatever is capable of definition must be defined."[65] Thus, good is transcendental in nature, at least in the sense that we cannot grasp it in its entirety, or define all its variations and forms as good itself. It recedes beyond every attempt of specification either in language or action. The spiritual *noumenon* is inaccessible to us, whether empirically, rationally, or otherwise. And yet, when we meet with some particular good, when the *fainomenon* appears, we recognize it or feel it.[66] In this sense, it is like the Sun—we cannot see it, but we do see things by its light.[67] Thus, everything begins—in moral education—with wonder and humility.

Second—the question of the origin of good has an answer.[68] It is an old, fundamental, but in no way banal, question. Where does good come from? Plato offered his answer in an unforgettable way in traditional Western thought, through the famous dialogue between Socrates and Euthyphro (also known as Euthyphro's dilemma).[69] The narrative contours of the dialogue are beautiful. Socrates and Euthyphro meet by chance on the way to the Royal Office, where complaints are lodged against citizens who in

---

63. A philosophical statement explaining that whatever is finite cannot fully incorporate or comprehend the infinite, let alone define it.

64. On the problematic definition of the terms good and evil, see the timeless reflections of C. S. Lewis. For example, "You can be good for the mere sake of goodness: you cannot be bad for the mere sake of badness. You can do a kind action when you are not feeling kind and when it gives you no pleasure, simply because kindness is right; but no one ever did a cruel action simply because cruelty is wrong, but only because cruelty was pleasant or useful to him. In other words, badness cannot succeed even in being bad in the same way in which goodness is good. Goodness is, so to speak, itself: badness is only spoiled goodness. And there must be something good first before it can be spoiled." Lewis, *Mere Christianity*, 38.

65. Moore, *Principia ethica*, 1.10. Citation is from the online version.

66. The traditional description of reality: noumenal—reality as it is; phenomenal—reality as it is revealed to us.

67. Cf. his light metaphors in Comenius, *Way of Light.*

68. The following paragraphs concerning the origin of the good are inspired by Peter Kreeft, *Návrat.*

69. Cf. Plato, *Euthyfrón.*

some way have violated the religious laws of the *polis*. Socrates comes as a defendent—as I recall, it was for his impiety. Euthyphro comes with his own case as a plaintiff—he wants to sue his father for inadvertantly killing a slave. Socrates wonders very much about his intentions, since the Greeks generally considered respect for parents as a manifestation of piety, and asks Euthyfro to teach him exactly what piety is—it would be useful for him when his own case came up (beautiful irony!). Euthyphro's answer, which I have abbreviated and paraphrased, is: to act as the gods do, to imitate them, do what they do, say what they say, love what they love. And, because in the sacred texts there is a story where a divine son (Dias) acts against his father, Euthyphro considers his own behavior as pious. Socrates responds with the question whether piety means imitating every god, or only some. Euthyphro's first answer is, all of them. Socrates, however, challenges this belief by pointing to the fact that different gods do and say different things which are often completely contradictory. To imitate all the gods would mean to behave in a contradictory way—what is pious for one is not pious for another. Euthyphro is in a tight spot, but Socrates doesn't let up and asks another question that is key to our theme of the origin and essence of the good: is good (and godliness) good because the gods say it, or do the gods say it because it is good? Is something good because the gods will it, or do they will it because it is good? In other words, do the gods determine what is good, or does what is good determine who the gods are? Euthyphro is confused. But then he assumes the position that the good is good because the gods say it. Socrates objects: If any act were good only because the gods said it, that would mean that the good is arbitrary and the gods are capricious. If, for example, a god said that eating the ears of your neighbor was good, would it be good? Then piety would mean that the gods should be obeyed, not because they are good, but simply because they require it.

The opposite of the moral capriciousness of the gods is when it is they who are dependent—if the good determined the gods, it would follow that the gods are in a subordinate position to an entity which is greater than them. Good would be the standard, according to which the gods themselves would be judged (by human reason). But what then would become of the gods? That is exactly what Socrates does—he judges the gods of the Greeks. Also, what he wants to say in his singularly humorous way, not only to Euthyphron, is that the Greek gods are ungodly. Inconsistent and often immoral. Are they not, in the end, our own projections? The personification of humanity? Fantasy? The Athenians didn't like it.

Comenius's concepts of good, the content of piety and the form of spirituality are different. And that is because his God is different. He is neither superior nor subordinate to good. He does not determine good arbitrarily, nor is it subject to any moral standard. That is because Godness is goodness. To hyperbolize, God doesn't have His Ten Commandments on the wall at home so every evening He can examine His conscience—today was okay, today I was a good God . . . Comenius's concepts of the nature of God and the good are the same. They have one nature. Godness is goodness. The *summum bonum*. Whatever is good, is divine and sacred. That is why human participation in the good brings such unique pleasure—every good act means touching divine reality. The more often people touch this reality, the more it becomes their own. By virtue of the good, individuals themselves become more real (ontologically)—the more they are good, the more they *are*. The more people are what they should be, the more humane they become. And vice versa, the worse people are (morally), the less real they are, the less human, until they can become a complete phantom or an "unman," as Comenius puts it.[70] So much for Comenius's meta-ethics. It is embedded in the absolute—ontologically and morally—in God, i.e., in that being of which it is impossible to think any better.

Third—if Comenius is right, that people have "engraved" somewhere "in their heart" some kind of spiritual organ or sensor of good, it follows that they also have an authentic spiritual need for the good—in addition to physical, mental, etc. needs. We have seen that humanity is fragile, threatened on every side—by the variability of the environment, unstable conditions, but most of all by its own finitude. At the same time, the fundamental need of the human self, which comes with existence, is the need for security, stability, or anchoring. The spiritual *I* is secured in two ways.

A. First, by the fact that *I am seen*, I am noticed, watched, and cared for. The basis of human identity is laid when my existence is reflected in the eyes of someone else, both intimately and permanently. Children discover that they *are*, when someone notices them, notices and perceives them. If no one notices a child, it will not exist, it will not survive—literally, biologically. If someone feeds a child but never looks at them, if their presence is not felt by someone, their sense of self will be

---

70. The phrase in Czech is *aby člověk neupadal v nečlověka*, that is "man regressing to unman" (*Pampaedia*, II:8). Interestingly, C. S. Lewis uses the very same word, "unman," when describing the "abolition of man." See his final book of the cosmic trilogy, *That Hideous Strength*.

lost, or very unstable (mentally and spiritually). If, on the other hand, a child receives deep and permanent attention, they learn on the one hand that they *are*, they exist, and on the other hand that they are worthy of attention, valuable, important, and accepted.

B. The human self is further provided for by *belonging* to someone other than themselves. Human life is such that both the newborn and the adult need to belong to someone, to belong—again, intimately and permanently. It is a need which is fundamentally human. If individuals don't belong to someone, their identity is threatened. They don't know who they are. Which is a state that cannot be sustained long term, either psychologically or ontologically.

According to Comenius, there is obviously something wrong with the human world, because to a greater or lesser degree we all experience the continual frustration of these fundamental needs—in the first case we experience the feeling that no one notices us, or perhaps, not as much as we need; we feel overlooked. In the second case, we don't have, or don't know, someone to belong to, someone to give ourselves to wholly, intimately, permanently, because we repeatedly (sometimes permanently) are disappointed by others. Perhaps we experience that we ourselves are disappointing others, we are incapable of giving ourselves in the way we would like to.

The human self can also be frustrated by the deprivation of other needs as well, making it more difficult to experience the fullness of its being, but the need to be seen and to belong, from the moral point of view, seems to be essential. If these needs are not fulfilled, the human self tends to expand, to enlarge its presence; it becomes more visible, so as to be noticed. The person begins to use other people as a mirror in which to be seen. In the life struggle for importance they manipulate others, so those others will react to their request for confirmation of their worth. But this ruins any authentic interpersonal relationship, because the other is treated as an object. *I—it*, instead of *I—you*, to put it in Martin Buber's terms. The interpersonal relationship is falsified—I see only a reflection of myself in the other. Instead of the unselfish "I belong to you," or "I'm here for you," what appears is the dehumanizing, because usurping, "you belong to me." Instead of me noticing (valuing) you, it's me watching (suspiciously) you. The tragedy of this state is that the more the human self expands in order to be noticed, the less worthy of notice it is. The more it wants to get for itself, the more it loses. The more preoccupied with itself, the less human it is.

In the seventeenth century Comenius called this *samosvojnost*, in the twentieth century, Craig R. Dykstra called it "moral egocentricity" with reference to Marcel.[71] It is a tendency that everyone suffers from, to one degree or another. At the same time, we all have the need to be seen and to belong. Sometimes we serve each other and thus fulfill this need, but very often we don't. We have some idea of fulfilling it, if we have had a positive experience in this respect and we know what it's like when someone gives us attention, care, love and devotion, especially when we don't have to ask for it. But the problem is that the others themselves are imperfect, not so often stable, often contradictory and above all, finite. Just like me.

But the needs of seeing/belonging call for fulfillment and cannot be suppressed or replaced by any substitute. This is where spirituality enters the discussion. Faith—as Comenius understands it—is not an irrational superstition or fanatical passion, but an almost somatic conviction that I am fully seen or regarded, noticed, and yet (surprisingly) loved—intimately and permanently. By the Creator, God, and not just any god: Comenius's divine instance is, as we have seen, the *summum bonum*, but at the same time, a personal being. Viktor Frankl speaks in passing of the *summa persona bona*.[72] One can belong to such a being fundamentally, personally, safely. If there is any hope for overcoming our *samosvojnost*, our bent into ourselves, then, according to Comenius, it is through just such a secure identity. I know about my own self-centered tendencies, my own "sin," Comenius would say, and I know that even so I am loved, and I know to whom I belong. What is important, I stress again, is this relationship—personal, intimate, loving. In such a relationship, a person has the good, that is, truly internalized, a good reason to strive for the knowledge of what is good, and also a reason to want the good and to do good, even if no person is looking.

I close this meditation on ethical education with a reference to Comenius, because his concept presents a unique synthesis of philosophical, anthropological, and pedagogical principles which have proven to be

---

71. Dykstra, *Vision*, 48.

72. Frankl's concept of "sense" is very close to Comenius's. In an interview with Lapide he expresses a number of anthropological and ethical ideas which would surely please Comenius. For example, "Self-realization is only possible when I lose myself, forget myself, overlook myself. Because to realize myself I must have some reason to do so. And that means I surrender myself to some thing or person . . . It is the same as with happiness and joy. If I have no reason for happiness, I cannot be happy; when I try to be happy, I lose everything that would, in my eyes, be reasons for happiness." Frankl, *Bůh a člověk*, 47–48.

functional, and in large part timeless. Comenius's concept comes out of a realistic anthropology, neither overvaluing nor undervaluing the person. Neither romanticizing nor damning. It recognizes human potential, but also understands human weakness and frailty. It develops the positive potential, and teaches the overcoming of negative tendencies—to acknowledge, forgive, and relinquish. Its philosophical understanding of "human affairs" enables it to cultivate ethics on the individual, social, and meta-ethical levels, that is, it cultivates respect for the sacred (transcendental), respect for one's neighbor and for oneself. Comenius is also clear about the teachability of virtue—instilling virtue is not indoctrination, but a matter of course, and instilling it should not happen only on the cognitive level (knowing the good), but also on the volitional and affective levels (to want the good, to love the good), as well as the level of performance (to do the good), and behind it all is the spiritual relationship to the sacred (even when no one is looking).

Comenius's starting point is, of course, far from the modern or postmodern view. I think, however, that the crisis of the (post)modern paradigm that we have witnessed for some time opens the way for new, interpretive horizons in relation to concepts from pre-modern thinking.[73] Not everything that is old must necessarily be old-fashioned.[74] Comenius's concept of ethical education is without doubt old and unfashionable, but in the context of the current state of (post)modern ethics, the question is whether that isn't its greatest advantage.

73. Stephen Toulmin illustrates the crisis of modernity with a picture. He suggests the trajectory of modern philosophy in the shape of the Greek letter omega. It means that despite the success in experimental and technical areas, the philosophic questions pertaining to the meaning of the final order of things remain, unresolved. After about three hundred years we are back at the beginning; we haven't gotten very far. See Toulmin, *Cosmopolis*, 167.

74. This approach was a great way for C. S. Lewis to describe his concept of *chronological snobbery*. He defines it as "uncritical acceptance of the intellectual climate common to our own age and the assumption that whatever has gone out of date is on that account discredited." See Lewis, *Surprised*, 206.

Bibliography

Allen, R. T. "Rational Autonomy: The Destruction of Freedom." *Journal of Philosophy of Education* 16 (1982) 199–207.

Alt, Robert. *Pokrokový charakter Komenského pedagogiky.* Prague: Státní pedagogické nakladatelství, 1959.

Anzenbacher, Arno. *Úvod do etiky.* Prague: Zvon, 1994.

Aquinas, Thomas. *The Summa Theologica.* Accessed June 29, 2018. http://www.documentacatholicaomnia.eu/03d/1225-1274,_Thomas_Aquinas,_Summa_Theologiae_%5B1%5D,_EN.pdf.

Aristotle. *Nicomachean Ethics.* Translated by W. D. Ross. http://classics.mit.edu/Aristotle/nicomachaen.2.ii.html.

Aronson, Elliot. *Social Animal.* New York: Worth, 2011.

Atherton, Thomas. *A Critique of Lawrence Kohlberg's Theories of Moral Development and Moral Education.* PhD diss., Boston University, 1979.

Bacon, Francis. *Nové organon.* Prague: Svoboda, 1974.

Bauer, Gary. "The Moral of the Story: How to Teach Values in the Nation's Classrooms." *Heritage Foundation Policy Review* 38 (1986) 26.

Bauman, Zygmunt. *Individualizovaná společnost.* Prague: Mladá fronta, 2004.

Barrow, Robin and Ronald Woods. *An Introduction to Philosophy of Education.* New York: Routledge, 1988.

Bělohradský, Václav. *Společnost nevolnosti.* Prague: Slon, 2007.

Bennett, William J. *The Book of Virtues.* First edition. New York: Simon and Schuster, 1993.

Benson, Thomas. L. "The Forms of Indoctrinatory Method." In *Philosophy of Education 1977: Proceedings of the Thirty-third Annual Meeting of the Philosophy of Education Society,* 333–43. Worcester, MA: Philosophy of Education Society, 1977.

Brázda, Radim. *Úvod do srovnávací etiky.* Prague: KLP, 1998.

Čapek, Robert. *Odměny a tresty ve školní praxi.* Prague: Grada, 2008.

Čapková, Dagmar. "On the Impact of J. A. Comenius to the Theory and Practice of Education." In *Symposium Comenianum 1982,* 11–22. Uherský Brod: Comenius Museum, 1984.

Chapman, Richard. A., ed. *Etika ve veřejné službě pro nové tisíciletí.* Prague: SLON, 2003.

Chesterton, G. K. *Ortodoxie.* Prague: Academia, 1992.

Cipro, Miroslav. *Prameny výchovy, Galerie světových pedagogů I, II, III.* Prague: M. Cipro, 2002.

Comenius, Jan Amos. *Didaktika analytická.* Prague: Samcovo knihkupectví, 1946.

———. *Didaktika česká.* 4.ed. Prague: I. L. Kober, 1937.

———. *Didactica magna.* In *Dílo Jana Amose Komenského* 15, edited by Milan Kopecký, 35-214. Prague: Academia, 1986.

———. *Didaktika velká.* Prague: Grégr a syn, 1905.

———. *The Great Didactic.* Translated by Maurice Walter Keatinge. London: Black, 1896.

———. *Hlubina bezpečnosti.* Prague: Spolek Komenského, 1927.

———. *Methodus linguarum novissima.* In *Vybrané spisy Jana Amose Komenského* 6.15/ II, 91-361. Czech translation by J. Šmahy. Prague: Státní Pedagogické Nakladatelství Prague, 1966.

———. *Obecná porada o nápravě věcí lidských,* 1, 2, 3. Prague: Nakladatelství Svoboda, 1992.

———. *Opera didactica omnia,* IV. Prague: Státní pedagogické nakladatelství, 1955.

———. *Orbis sensualium pictus.* Beroun: Machart, 2012.

———. *The Way of Light.* Translated by E. T. Campagnac. London: Hodder and Stoughton, 1938.

Crittenden, Brian. S. "Indoctrination as Mis-education." In *Concepts of Indoctrination,* edited by Ivan A. Snook. London: Routledge & Kegan Paul, 1972.

Dacík, Reginald M. *Mravouka.* Olomouc: Dominikánská edice Krystal, 1946.

Danišková, Zuzana. "Marx opäť v školách: Multikultúrna výchova ako nástroj lepšej spoločnosti." *Pedagogický časopis* 1 (2010) 58–75.

Dearden, R. F. "Autonomy and Education." In *Education and Development of Reason,* edited by R. F. Dearden, et al. London: Routledge & Kegan Paul, 1972.

———. "Autonomy as an Educational Ideal." In *Philosophers Discuss Education,* edited by S. C. Brown. London: Macmillan, 1975.

DeVries, Rheta and Betty Zan. *Moral Classrooms, Moral Children: Creating a Constructivist Atmosphere in Early Education.* New York: Teachers College Press, 1994.

Dinkmeyer, Don, et al. *The Parent's Handbook: Systematic Training for Effective Parenting.* Circle Pines, MN: American Guidance Service, 1997.

Downey, Meriel, and A. V. Kelly. *Moral Education: Theory and Practice.* London: Harper and Row, 1978.

Durkheim, Émile. *Moral Education: A Study in the Theory and Application of the Sociology of Education.* Translated by Everett K. Wilson and Herman Schnurer. Glencoe, IL: Free Press, 1961.

———. *Sociologie a filosofie.* Translated by Danuše Navrátilová and Zdeněk Strmiska. Prague: Sociologické nakladatelství, 1998.

Dykstra, Craig R. *Vision and Character: A Christian Educator's Alternative to Kohlberg.* New York: Paulist, 1981.

Erickson, Millard J. *Truth or Consequences: The Promise and Perils of Postmodernism.* Downers Grove, IL: InterVarsity, 2001.

Ethical Forum of the Czech Republic. *Na cestě s etickou výchovou.* Kroměříž: Luxpress, 2004.

Fineman, Howard. "The Virtuecrats." *Newsweek* 13 (June 1993) 36.

Finkielkraut, Alain. *Destrukce myšlení.* Brno: Atlantis, 1993.

Flew, Antony. "Indoctrination and doctrines." In *Concepts of Indoctrination,* edited by I. A. Snook, 67–92. London: Routledge & Kegan Paul, 1972.

———. "Indoctrination and religion." In *Concepts of Indoctrination,* edited by I. A. Snook, 106–16. London: Routledge & Kegan Paul, 1972b.

Foucault, Michel. *Dohlížet a trestat. Kniha o zrodu vězení.* Prague: Dauphin, 2000.

Frankl, Viktor. E. and P. Lapide. *Bůh a člověk hledající smysl.* Brno: Cesta, 2011.

Fuchs, Eric. *Co dělá naše jednání dobrým?* Jihlava: Mlýn, 2003.

Furger, Franz. *Etika seberealizace, osobních vztahů a politiky.* Prague: Academia, 2003.

Gardner, Peter. "Religious Upbringing and the Liberal Ideal of Religious Autonomy." *Journal of Philosophy of Education* 22 (1988) 89–105.

Gilligan, Carol. *In a Different Voice: Psychological Theory and Women's Development.* Cambridge: Harvard University Press, 1982.

Glasser, William. *School Without Failure.* New York: Harper and Row, 1969.

Guroian, Vigen. *Tending the Heart of Virtue: How Classic Stories Awaken a Child's Moral Imagination.* Oxford: Oxford University Press, 2002.

Green, Thomas F. "Indoctrination and beliefs." In *Concepts of Indoctrination*, edited by I. A. Snook, 25–46. London: Routledge & Kegan Paul, 1972.

Greer, Thomas H. and Gavin Lewis, *A Brief History of the Western World*, 7th edition, Florida: Harcourt Brace & Comp, 1997.

Gregory, I. M. M., and R. G. Woods. "Indoctrination: inculcating doctrines." In *Concepts of Indoctrination*, edited by I. A. Snook, 162–89. London: Routledge & Kegan Paul, 1972.

Grenz, Stanley J. *A Primer on Postmodernism.* Grand Rapids: Eerdmans, 1996.

Hábl, Jan. *Teaching and Learning Through Story. Comenius' Labyrinth and the Educational Potential of Narrative Allegory.* Bonn: Culture and Science, 2014.

———. *Ultimate Human Goals in Comenius and Modern Pedagogy.* Gaudeamus: Hradec Králové, 2011.

Halstead, J. Mark. *The Case for Muslim Voluntary-aided Schools: Some Philosophical Reflections.* Cambridge: The Islamic Academy, 1986.

Hare, R. M. "Adolescents into Adults." In *Aims in Education: The Philosophic Approach*, edited by T. H. B. Hollins, 47–70. Manchester: Manchester University Press, 1964.

Hare, William. *Open-mindedness and Education.* Kingston and Montreal: McGill-Queen's University Press, 1979.

Haškovcová, Helena. *Lékařská etika.* Prague: Galén, 2002.

Haworth, Lawrence. *Autonomy: An Essay in Philosophical Psychology and Ethics.* New Haven and London: Yale University Press, 1986.

Haydon, Graham. "Autonomy as an Aim of Education and Autonomy of Teachers." *Journal of Philosophy of Education* 17 (1983) 219–28.

Hirst, Paul H. *Knowledge and the Curriculum: A Collection of Philosophical Papers.* London: Routledge & Kegan Paul, 1974.

Hobbes, Thomas. *Leviathan.* Online version of the text from 1651, Accessed January 10, 2015. http://www.earlymoderntexts.com/assets/pdfs/hobbes1651part1_2. pdf#page=1&zoom=auto,-229,445.

Holmes, Arthur. F. *Ethics. Approaching Moral Decisions.* Downer's Grove: InterVarsity, 1984.

Honneth, Axel. *Sociální filosofie a postmoderní etika.* Prague: Filosofia, 1996.

Hull, John M. *Studies in Religion and Education.* London: Falmer, 1984.

Hunter, James Davison. *Death of Character: Moral Education in an Age Without Good and Evil.* New York: Basic, 2000.

Illich, Ivan. *Deschooling Society.* New York: Harper and Row, 1970.

Johnson, Thomas K. *Christian Ethics in Secular Cultures.* Bonn: Culture and Science, 2014.

Kant, Imanuel. *O výchově.* Translated by Josef Jančařík. Prague: 1931.

Kazepides, Tasos. "Indoctrination, Doctrines and Foundations of Rationality." In *Philosophy of Education 1987: Proceedings of the Forty-third Annual Meeting of the Philosophy of Education Society*, edited by Barbara Arnstine and Donald Arnstine. Normal: Philosophy of Education Society, 1987.

Kilpatrick, William. *Why Johnny Can't Tell Right from Wrong: Moral Illiteracy and the Case for Character Education.* Simon & Schuster, 1992.

Kirschenbaum, Howard. *Advanced Value Clarification.* La Jolla, CA: Calif. University Associates, 1977.

Kohák, Erazim. *Člověk, dobro a zlo. O smyslu života v zrcadle dějin: Kapitoly z dějin morální filosofie.* Prague: Ježek, 1993.

Kohlberg, Lawrence. *Essays on Moral Development II. The psychology of moral development.* San Francisco: Harper & Row, 1984.

———. "The Just Community Approach to Moral Education in Theory and Practice." In *Moral Education: Theory and Application*, edited by Marvin W. Berkowitz and Fritz Oser, 27–88. London: Lawrence Erlbaum Associates, 1985.

Kohn, Alfie. "How Not to Teach Values: A Critical Look at Character Education." *Phi Delta Kappa* 78 (February 1997) 1–19.

———. "The Truth About Self-esteem." *Phi Delta Kappa* 76 (December 1994) 272–83.

Kolář, Petr and Vladimír Svoboda. *Logika a etika. Úvod do meta-etiky.* Prague: Filosofia, 1997.

Kožmín, Zdeněk and Drahomíra Kožmínová. *Zvětšeniny z Komenského.* Brno: Host 2007.

Krasnovskij, Archip Aleksejevič. *Jan Amos Komenský.* Prague: Státní pedagogické nakladatelství, 1955.

Kratochvíl, Ladislav. "Pedagogický realismus Komenského." In *Jan Amos Komenský*, edited by Jiří Vaclav Klíma, 123–31. Prague: L. J. Peroutka, Unie, 1947.

Kreeft, Peter. *Making Choices. Practical Wisdom for Everyday Moral Decisions.* Ann Arbor, MI: Servant, 1990.

———. *Návrat ke ctnostem.* Prague: Krystal OP, 2013.

Kulič, Vaclav. "J. A. Comenius and Contemporary Psychodidactics." In *Symposium Comenianum 1982*, edited by Marie Kyralová and Jana Přivratská. 122–31. Uherský Brod: Comenius Institute of Education of the Czechoslovak Academy of Sciences. 1984.

Langová, Marta and Marie Vacínová. *Jak se to chováš?!* Prague: Empatie 1994.

Lencz, Ladislav and Olga Křížová. *O Etická výchova—metodický material 1, 2, 3.* Prague: Luxpress, 2000.

Lewis, C. S. *The Abolition of Man, or Reflections on Education with Special Reference to the Teaching of English in the Upper Forms of Schools.* New York: Touchstone, 1996.

———. *Mere Christianity.* New York: Macmillan, 1981, česky: *K jádru křesťanství*, Prague: Návrat domů, 1993.

———. *Pilgrims Regress.* Grand Rapids: Erdmans, 1996.

———. *Surprised by Joy: The Shape of my Early Life.* New York: Harcourt, Brace, Jovanovich, 1955.

Lickona, Thomas. *Educating for Character: How Our Schools Can Teach Respect and Responsibility.* New York: Bantam, 1992.

Lipovetsky, Gilles. *Soumrak povinnosti. Bezbolestná etika nových demokratických časů.* Prague: Prostor, 1999.

Loevinger, Jane. *Ego Development.* San Francisco: Jossey-Bass, 1976.

Lorenzová, Jitka. "O smyslu profesní etiky učitelství." In *Smysl, cíl a účel ve výchově, umění a sportu (Filosofická reflexe lidského jednání)*, edited by Naděžda Pelcová, et al., 92–108. Prague: Univerzita Karlova v Praze, Pedagogická fakulta, 2012.

Lyotard, Jean-François. *O postmodernismu*. Prague: Filosofie, 1993.

MacIntyre, Alisdair. *After Virtue*, third edition. University of Notre Dame Press, 2007.

———. *Ctnosti*. Prague:Oikoymenh, 2004.

Marklund, Sixten. *School Stages and Student Development: An Application of Comenian Thinking*. In *Symposium Comenianum 1982*, edited by Marie Kyralová and Jana Přivratská, 55–63. Uherský Brod: Comenius Institute of Education of the Czechoslovak Adademy of Sciences, 1984.

Maslow, Abraham H. "Psychological Data and Value Theory." In *New Knowledge in Human Values*, edited by Abraham H. Maslow and P. Sorokin, 119–36. New York: Harper and Row, 1959.

———. *The Psychology of Science*. New York: Harper and Row, 1966.

McLaughlin, T. H. "Parental Rights and the Religious Upbringing of Children." *Journal of Philosophy of Education* 19 (1984) 75–83.

Menck, Peter. "The Formation of Conscience: A Lost Topic of Didactic." *Journal of Curriculum Studies* 33 (2001) 261–75.

Milgram, Stanley. *Obedience to Authority: An Experimental View*. New York: Harper Collins, 2004.

Moore, George Edward. *Principia ethica*.1903. Online English version accessed April 10, 2015. http://fair-use.org/g-e-moore/principia-ethica.

Moore, Willis. "Indoctrination and democratic method." In *Concepts of Indoctrination*, edited by I. A. Snook, 93–100. London: Routledge & Kegan Paul, 1972.

Morris, Thomas V. *Making Sense of It All: Pascal and the Meaning of Life*. Grand Rapids: Eerdmans, 1992.

Neill, A. S. *Summerhill: A Radical Approach to Child Rearing*. New York: Hart, 1960.

Nováková, Marie, et al. *Učíme etickou výchovu*. Prague: Luxpress, 2006.

Nullens, Patrick and Ronald T. Michener. *The Matrix of Christian Ethics: Integrating Philosophy and Moral Theology in a Postmodern Context*. Downers Grove, IL: InterVarsity Press, 2010.

O'Leary, Paul T. "The Indoctrinated State of Mind." In *Philosophy of Education 1979: Proceeding of the Thirty-Fifth Annual Meeting of the Philosophy of Education Society*, edited by Jerrold R. Coombs, 66–76. Normal, IL: Philosophy of Education Society, 1979.

Page, Ralph C. "Towards Some Serious Entertaining." In *Philosophy of Education 1985: Proceedings of the Forty-First Annual Meeting of the Philosophy of Education Society*, edited by David Nyberg, 107–10. Normal, IL: Philosophy of Education Society, 1985.

Palouš, Radim. *Čas výchovy*. Prague: Státní pedagogické nakladatelství, 1991.

———. *Komenského Boží svět*. Prague: Státní pedagogické nakladatelství, 1992.

Pascal, Blaise. *Pensées*. Translated by A. J. Krailsheimer. New York: Penguin, 1995.

Passmore, John. "On Teaching to be Critical." In *The Concept of Education*, edited by R. S. Peters, 193–203. London: Routledge & Kegan Paul, 1967.

Patočka, Jan. *Komeniologické studie I*. Prague: Oikoymenh, 1997.

Pelcová, Naděžda. "Druhý život Komenského." In *Paideia* 3/4, IX (2012) 1–11.

Peshkin, Alan. *God's Choice: The Total World of a Fundamentalist Christian School*. Chicago: The University of Chicago Press, 1986.

Pešková, Jaroslava. "Aktuální aspekty filosofické argumentace v Komenského, Konsultaci."' *Filosofický časopis* 40 (1992), 51–56.

Peters, Richard Stanley. *Authority, Responsibility and Education.* London: Allen and Unwin, 1973.

Petříček, Miroslav. *Úvod do současné filosofie.* Prague: Herman & Synové, 1997.

Philips, Adam. *On fFirtation: Psychoanalytic Essays on the Uncommitted Life.* Cambridge, MA: Harvard University Press, 1994.

Piaget, Jean. *Jan Amos Comenius. Prospects* 23.1–2, 173–96. UNESCO: International Bureau of Education, 1993. Online version at http://www.ibe.unesco.org/sites/default/files/comeniuse.pdf.

———. *The Moral Judgment of the Child.* London: Kegan Paul, 1932.

Plato. *Euthyfrón, Obrana Sókrata, Kritón.* Prague: Oikoymenh, 2005.

———. *Euthydémos, Menón.* Translated by František Novotný. Prague: Oikoymenh, 2000.

Plesu, Andrei. *Minima moralia: poznámky k etike interval* [Minimal morality: notes on the ethics of the gap]. Translated from the Romanian original by Jana Páleníková. Bratislava: Kalligram, 2001.

Podolská, Bohuslava. "Prosociální výchova." *Učitelské noviny* 18 (2008), accessed online January 10, 2015. http://www.ucitelskenoviny.cz/?archiv&clanek=1091.

Popelová, Jiřina. *Komenského cesta k všenápravě.* Prague: Státní Pedagogické Nakladatelství, 1958.

Power, F. Clark. "Democratic Schools and the Problem of Moral Authority." In *Handbook of Moral Behavior and Development 3*, edited by William M. Kurtines and Jacob L Gewirtz, 187–98. Hillsdale, NJ: Lawrence Earlbaum Associates, 1991.

Power, F. Clark, et al. *Lawrence Kohlberg's Approach to Moral Education.* New York: Columbia University Press, 1989.

Příkaský, Jiljí V. *Učebnice základů etiky.* Kostelní Vydří: Karmelitánské nakladatelství, 2000.

Raths, Louis E., et al. *Values and Teaching.* Second edition. Columbus, OH: Merrill, 1978.

Rokeach, Milton. *The Open and Closed Mind: Investigations into the Nature of Belief Systems and Personality Systems.* New York: Basic, 1960.

Roche-Olivar, Roberto. *Etická výchova.* Bratislava: Orbis Pictus Istropolitana, 1992.

Rogers, Carl. *On Becoming a Person.* Boston: Houghton-Mifflin, 1961.

Rousseau, John Jacques. *Emil, čili o vychování.* Translated by Jaroslav Novák and Milan Svoboda. Prague: Dědictví Komenského, 1911.

Jean-Paul Sartre, *Existentialism Is Humanism.* Translated by Carol Macomber. New Haven: Yale University Press, 2007.

Schaeffer, Francis A. *How Should We Then Live? The Rise and Decline of Western Thought and Culture.* London: Marshall, Morgan & Scott, 1980.

Schirrmacher, Thomas. *Leadership and Ethical Responsibility: The Three Aspects of Every Decision.* Bonn: Culture and Science, 2013.

Scruton, Roger et al. *Education and Indoctrination: An Attempt at Definition and a Review of Social and Political Implications.* Middlesex: Education Research Centre, 1985.

Sedláčková, Markéta. *Důvěra a demokracie. Přehled sociologických teorií důvěry od Tocquevilla po transformaci v postkomunistických zemích.* Prague: Slon, 2012.

Simon, Sidney B., et al. *Values Clarification: A Handbook of Practical Strategies for Teachers and Students.* New York: Hart Publishing, 1972.)

Snook, Ivan. A. *Indoctrination and Education.* London: Routledge & Kegan Paul, 1972.

Sokol, Jan. *Etika, život, instituce. Pokus o praktickou filosofii.* Prague: Vyšehrad, 2014.

Sokol, Jan and Zdeněk Pinc. *Antropologie a etika*. Prague: Triton 2003.

Sommers, Christina Hoff. "Teaching the Virtues." *The Public Interest* 111 (1993) 3–13.

Spiecker, Ben. "Indoctrination, Intellectual Virtues and Rational Emotions." *Journal of Philosophy of Education* 21 (1987) 261–66.

Srogoň, Tomáš. "Comenius's Basic Principles of Teaching and Present-Day Didactics." In *Symposium Comenianum 1982*, edited by Marie Kyralová and Jana Přivratská, 109–13. Uherský Brod: Comenius Museum, 1984.

Strouhal, Martin. "K morálním a pedagogickým aspektům Durkheimova pojetí socializace." *Pedagogický časopis/Journal of Pedagogy* 1 (2010) n.p.

———. "Několik poznámek k teorii morální výchovy Emila Durkheima." In *Historie a perspektivy didaktického myšlení*, edited by Alena Vališová, 88–104. Prague: Karolinum, 2005.

Sutor, Bernhard. *Politická etika*. Prague: Oikoymenh, 1996

Švarcová, Eva. "Možnosti etické výchovy ovlivnit vztahy ve skupině." In *Humanizace ve výchově a vzdělávání*. *Východiska, možnost a meze*, edited by Jan Hábl and Jana Doležalová, 144–50. Fakulta pedagogická UHK, Gaudeamus, 2010.

Thalburg, Irving. "Socialization and Autonomous Behaviour." *Tulane Studies in Philosophy* 28 (1979) 21–37.

Thiessen, Elmer John. *Teaching for Commitment Liberal Education, Indoctrination, and Christian Nurture*. McGill-Queen's University Press, 1993.

Tichý, František Rut. "S J. A. Komenským do budování socialistické školy." In *Jan Amos Komenský, Didaktické spisy*, edited by František Rut Tichý, 5–22. Prague: Státní Pedagogické Nakladatelství, 1951.

Toulmin, Stephen. *Cosmopolis, The hidden Agenda of Modernity*. Chicago: University of Chicago Press, 1990.

Vacek, Pavel. "K otázkám rozvoje prosociálnosti a altruismu." In *Socialia '97: Pomoc potřebným*, 105–14. Hradec Králové: Líp, 1998.

———. *Rozvoj morálního vědomí žáků. Metodické náměty k realizaci průřezových témat* Prague: Portál, 2008.

Vágnerová, Marie. *Psychologie školního dítěte*. Prague: Karolinum 1997.

Van Doren, Charles. *A History of Knowledge: Past, Present, and Future*. New York: Ballantine, 1991.

Ward, Keith. "Is Autonomy an Educational Ideal?" *Educational Analysis* 5 (1983) 47–55.

Welsch, Wolfgang. *Naše postmoderní moderna*. Prague: Zvon, 1994.

White, J. P. "Indoctrination without doctrines?" In *Concepts of Indoctrination*, edited by I. A. Snook, 190–201. London: Routledge & Kegan Paul, 1972.

Williams, Bernard. *Morality: An Introduction to Ethics*. New York (USA): Harper and Row, 1972.

Wilson, John. "Indoctrination and freedom." In *Concepts of Indoctrination*, edited by I. A. Snook, 101–5. London: Routledge & Kegan Paul, 1972.

———. "Education and Indoctrination." In *Aims in Education: The Philosophic Approach*, edited by T. H. B. Hollins, 24–46. Manchester: Manchester University Press, 1964.

Wright, Andrew. *Religion, Education and Postmodernity*. London: Routledge Falmer, 2004.

Zilcher, Ladislav and Jaroslav Říčan. "Multicultural Education as a Way to Inclusion." In *Internationalization in Teacher Education*, vol. 6, edited by Pia Maria Rabensteiner and Gerhard Rabensteiner, 192–207. Baltmannsweiler, Germany: Schneider, 2014.

Index of Names

Lightning Source UK Ltd.
Milton Keynes UK
UKHW04f1045131018
330445UK00001B/29/P